# *Haunted* LONDON

# *Haunted* LONDON

### DISCOVERING THE CITY'S BEST KEPT SECRETS

Richard Jones

METRO BOOKS

New York

**METRO BOOKS**
New York

An Imprint of Sterling Publishing
387 Park Avenue South
New York, NY 10016

METRO BOOKS and the distinctive Metro Books logo are trademarks of
Sterling Publishing Co., Inc.

Text © 2012 Richard Jones
Maps © 2012 New Holland Publishers (UK) Ltd
Maps are based on out of copyright Ordnance Survey Mapping
Illustrations © see page 192
© 2012 New Holland Publishers (UK) Ltd

Publisher: Aruna Vasudevan
Senior Editor: Charlotte Macey
Americanzier: Sally Mceachern
Designer: Colin Hall
Cover Design: Celeste Vlok
Cartographer: Bill Smuts
Production: Sarah Kulasek

ISBN 978-1-4351-3803-2

For information about custom editions, special sales, and premium
and corporate purchases, please contact Sterling Special Sales at
800-805-5489 or specialsales@sterlingpublishing.com

2 4 6 8 10 9 7 5 3 1

# CONTENTS

# INTRODUCTION

----London is one of the most haunted capital cities in the world. Its ghosts span many centuries and often illuminate dark corners of its brutal past. From those who perished inside England's most haunted building, the Tower of London, to the tragic victims of the famous serial killer Jack the Ripper, many of the phantoms that roam the capital are an essential part of British history, folklore, and legend.

London was founded by the Romans *c.*AD43 and, since their departure in AD410, centuries of demolition and rebuilding have seen the level of the city's streets rise by an amazing 28 feet (8.5 meters). Millions of people have lived and died in London and, as a consequence, there is not a patch of the old city that is not imbued with the memories and experiences of these former citizens.

There is an old saying that ghosts only ever appear in places that have known either great happiness or great misery, and London has certainly known both in abundance. But what exactly are ghosts?

The most frequent question I get asked is: *"Do you believe in ghosts?"* The answer has

to be an emphatic *"Yes."* There have, over the centuries, been too many accounts of ghosts and hauntings from honest, reliable, and publicity-shy people for them not to exist. I certainly do not believe that they are the dead coming back to haunt the living.

Indeed, the more I research and explore supernatural phenomena—and over the last 20 years I have traveled the length and breadth of Britain and Ireland visiting almost 2,000 haunted places—the more I become convinced that ghosts are little more than strong emotions that have somehow become imprinted upon their surroundings. I also believe that there are certain people who are more attuned to these "recordings" than the rest of us. This may be why ghosts can be so personal. There may be an entire group of people present when a haunting occurs and yet only a tiny minority of them might be lucky —or unlucky—enough to see the ghost.

Of course, hauntings can assume many different forms. It is, in fact, very rare for people to actually "see" a ghost. People sense them, smell them, feel them, and hear them, but a full-blown manifestation tends to be the exception rather than the rule.

In recent years, largely since the advent of digital cameras, there has been a sharp increase in the number of supposed ghost photographs, mostly consisting of "orbs." These floating balls of circular light are one of the most common types of alleged paranormal activity. Personally, I am very dubious about orbs and think there is nothing in the least bit ghostly about the majority of them. As John Mason—a professional photographer who is frequently on the road taking infrared film and digital images of haunted places—points out, orbs are mostly a product of the digital age. He believes them to be nothing more than light reflecting off particles of dust or moisture in the atmosphere; in other words they are physical rather than psychical objects.

But that aside, ghost stories are as popular today as they have ever been. In the pages that follow you will find a collection of more than 100 of London's most haunted locations divided by region. These are all accompanied by contact details, transport links, and maps so that you will be well-equipped to undertake your own ghostly research into the past.

Some of the stories are well known and have been handed down through the ages, while others here are much less well documented. Although I have tried, wherever possible, to offer historical corroboration for the events that led to some of the hauntings, I have set the stories down more or less as they were recounted by those who experienced them and I have made few attempts to explain them.

I hope that you enjoy the book and that you will take the opportunity to visit some, if not all, of the places included if you find yourself in London. And if it should happen that you encounter a ghost, then I would be delighted to hear of your experience.

Richard Jones, London
www.discovery-walks.com

## ⓘ information key

### Contact details

 Telephone number

Web site

### Transport links

 Underground station

 Overground station

# THEATERLAND & THE WEST END

The ghosts that roam the streets and buildings of London's West End are an eclectic mix. From England's most famous theater ghost "The Man in Gray" to the hidden horrors of what was once known as the most haunted house in London, the specters in this chapter cover all ages and all types. There are also a fair smattering of pubs with ghosts and even an underground station with its very own resident spook.

## HAUNTED LOCATIONS

1. Theatre Royal
2. Covent Garden Station
3. Lyceum Theatre
4. The Savoy
5. Theatre Royal
6. The Nell Gwynne
7. Adelphi Theatre
8. Langham Hilton Hotel
9. Coutts Bank
10. Duke of York's Theatre
11. Handel House Museum
12. John Snow
13. London Palladium
14. The Clermont Club
15. Burlington Arcade
16. Fortnum and Mason
17. 50 Berkeley Square

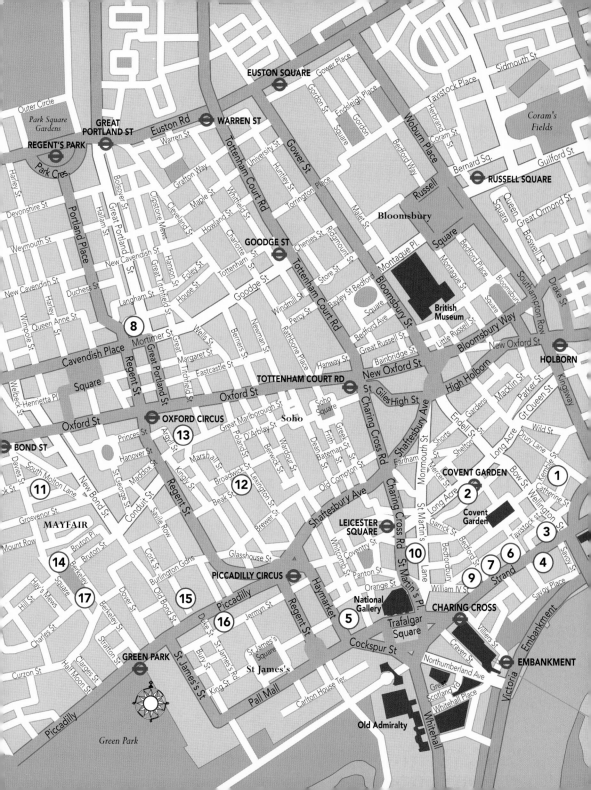

**10**

# THEATRE ROYAL
## CATHERINE STREET, WC2

See map p.9 ①

### ☞ THE CLOWN AND THE MAN IN GRAY

The Theatre Royal, Drury Lane, is the oldest working theater in London, and although the present building dates from 1812, the first theater on the site was founded in 1663.

Many phantoms are known to lurk in the wings behind its spectacular portico. One of these is the ghost of Joseph Grimaldi (see also page 49), whose character of the innocent, white-faced rogue became so universally popular that clowns are still known as "Joeys" in honor of the father of modern clownery. But the exertions of his craft exacted a terrible toll on Grimaldi's health and he was overcome by a crippling disease that forced him to abandon his profession. By 1818 the performer was destitute, and a benefit performance was organized at the Theatre Royal. Despite having to be carried onto the stage, and only able to perform seated, Grimaldi had lost none of his magic.

He died in 1837, but his ghost has returned to the theater many times and is renowned for administering a mischievous kick—actors, cleaners, and usherettes have all been on the receiving end of his spectral boot. One of Grimaldi's final wishes was that his head should be severed from his body prior to burial. This macabre request was apparently carried out, and this might account for the disembodied white face that has been seen around the theater.

Another of the theater's ghosts is that of "The Man in Gray," the limping apparition of a young man in a powdered wig, white ruffed shirt, gray riding cloak, and three-cornered hat. He invariably appears during daylight hours. In 1939, more than half the cast of the composer Ivor Novello's musical *The Dancing Years* were on stage for a photo call, when they witnessed the ghost cross the upper circle and melt into the wall.

The identity of "The Man in Gray" remains a mystery, although an intriguing discovery during renovations in the 1870s may shed some light onto what caused his ghost to haunt the theater. As workmen went about their business, they broke into a hidden room behind the wall into which the ghost vanishes. Inside they found the skeleton of a man. It was surrounded by

 *Drury Lane's Theatre Royal, where the ghosts of past actors refuse to take a final bow.*

remnants of gray cloth and had a dagger protruding from its ribcage. It has been speculated that the remains were those of a young man who had been murdered by his actress lover in a fit of jealous rage. His body was subsequently hidden in the secret recess, where it lay undiscovered until the Victorian renovation of the theater.

# (i) information

## Contact details

Theatre Royal
Catherine Street
London, WC2B 5JF

 **Theatre Royal site**
www.theatre-royal.com

## Transport links

⊖ Covent Garden

# COVENT GARDEN STATION
LONG ACRE, WC2                                    See map p.9 (2)

##  THE MAN IN THE HOMBURG HAT

On Christmas Eve 1955, ticket inspector Jack Hayden was writing up the log at Covent Garden Station, when the door of his office began to rattle violently. Thinking it was a lost late night reveler, Hayden called out: "There's no way through here," but the rattling grew more violent. The irritated inspector leapt to his feet and threw open the door. He found himself face to face with a tall man in a gray suit, wearing tight pants and sporting a Homburg hat. The man stared at Hayden without speaking, then turned, walked toward the stairway and seemingly melted into thin air.

Over the next few years, Hayden encountered the same apparition on no fewer than 40 occasions; the ghost was also seen by ticket collector Victor Locker.

London Underground called in spiritualist Eric Davey and a séance was held, after which Davey told *The Sunday Dispatch* newspaper: "I got the name Ter- something." Somebody suggested the name "Terris" and pictures of the Victorian actor William Terris were shown to Hayden and Locker, who had no doubt that he was the man they had seen.

Terris was murdered outside the Adelphi Theatre (see page 19) on December 16, 1897. His spectral appearances at Covent Garden Station have been explained by the fact that he was a frequent visitor to a baker's shop that had previously stood there.

◀ *The ghost of Victorian actor William Terris has been spotted frequently at Covent Garden Station.*

## (i) information

### Contact details

Covent Garden Station
41 Long Acre
Covent Garden
London, WC2E 9JT

☎ +44 (0)20 7222 1234

### Transport links

 Covent Garden

**14**

# LYCEUM THEATRE
## WELLINGTON STREET, WC2

See map p.9

###  THE SEVERED HEAD

In the late 19th century, the rafters of the Lyceum Theatre, now restored to its original opulent splendor by music impresario Lord Andrew Lloyd Webber, echoed to the thunderous applause of audiences that had come to marvel at the lavish Shakespearean productions staged here by actors Henry Irving and Ellen Terry.

One couple, however, had quite a shock in the 1880s when they happened to look over the balcony during an intermission and saw the severed head of a man leering up at them from a lady's lap in the stalls below!

Their curiosity aroused, they rose from their seats to investigate, but were forced to sit back down when the play resumed. During the second half of the performance, they kept looking over the railings, but the lady had a shawl over her lap. When the curtain came down, they raced downstairs and observed the lady leaving the theater. Unfortunately, they lost sight of her and were left to ponder the grisly enigma they had witnessed.

Some years later, the husband happened to visit a house in Yorkshire where, to his surprise, he saw a portrait of a man whose face was identical to that which he and his wife had seen in the lady's lap at the Lyceum. When he asked the owner of the house who the man was, he was told that it was a distant ancestor who had been beheaded for treason and whose family once owned the land on which the Lyceum now stands.

---

## ⓘ information

---

### Contact details

Lyceum Theatre
21 Wellington Street
London, WC2E 7RQ

☎ +44 (0)20 7420 8100

 **Lyceum site**
www.lyceum-theatre.co.uk

### Transport links

 Covent Garden

# THE SAVOY
STRAND, WC2

See map p.9 (4)

 KASPAR THE FELINE CHARM

Since it opened in 1889, The Savoy hotel has been synonymous with wealth and privilege. The actor Sir Henry Irving lived here; Edwardian millionaires thought nothing of flooding its courtyard with champagne; the Italian opera singer Enrico Caruso sang here and Hollywood actress Mae West claimed to have held conversations with her mother's ghost in one of its bedrooms.

In 1898, diamond king Joel Woolf held a dinner party at The Savoy, prior to his return to South Africa. It was noted that there were an unlucky 13 people seated at the table, but Woolf dismissed a comment by one of his guests that the first to leave the table would be the first to die. Indeed,

he made a point of being the first to rise to his feet and bid his fellow diners goodnight. Shortly afterward, he was shot dead in his office in Johannesburg.

Fearful that further parties of 13 might be deterred from booking a table, or even worse might suffer a similar fate, the management of The Savoy commissioned a wooden cat to be carved from a single piece of a London plane tree. They named the cat Kaspar, and ever since, should a party of 13 find themselves dining at The Savoy, another place is set at their table. With a white napkin tied around his neck, a resplendent Kaspar is brought to sit with the guests, and a saucer of milk is placed before him!

## (i) information

### Contact details
The Savoy
Strand
London, WC2R 0EU

 +44 (0)20 7836 4343

 Savoy site
www.fairmont.com/savoy

savoy@fairmont.com

### Transport links
Covent Garden;
Tottenham Court
Road; Holborn

# THEATRE ROYAL

SUFFOLK STREET, SW1

See map p.9 ⑤

## 👉 A MAN OF THE THEATER—EVEN IN DEATH

Celebrated British architect John Nash built the graceful and attractive Theatre Royal in 1821, and it saw its most successful period between 1853 and 1878, under the management of John Baldwin Buckstone. A popular actor and comedian, Buckstone was a great friend of the writer Charles Dickens. Indeed, Dickens once confessed that he had been so moved by Buckstone's performances when he was a boy that he had frequently gone home to "dream of his comicalities." Although Buckstone died in 1879, his ghost remained at the theater to which he had devoted 25 years of his life.

Many illustrious theatrical folk have seen Buckstone's spectral form at the theater. British actor Donald Sinden saw him while performing in *The Heiress* with fellow thespian Ralph Richardson in 1949. As he passed Richardson's dressing room one night, Sinden noticed a man in a long black coat looking out of the window with his back to him. Thinking it was his costar he called out "Goodnight Ralph" and continued on his way. It was then that he heard a familiar voice booming from the stage and realized that Richardson was still performing and could not, therefore, have been in his dressing room.

On other occasions, stagehands walking past what was once Buckstone's dressing room have clearly heard a voice rehearsing lines. However, on opening the door they have discovered nothing but an empty room.

In 1996, the theater launched a backstage tour and invited a group of VIP guests to join a rehearsal of the proposed route. An important inclusion was a visit to Buckstone's room, where participants would be treated to anecdotes about the man who had given so much to the theater. As the dry run began, the stage manager unlocked the room and went off to attend to other business. When the party arrived at Buckstone's room, the guide turned the handle and discovered that the door was locked. The mystified manager returned with the key, but no matter how hard he tried, he was unable to unlock it. Once the guests had departed, however, the door opened easily. Evidently Buckstone was not eager to welcome them into his former room!

 *Charles Dickens's great friend J. B. Buckstone still makes an occasional appearance at the Theatre Royal.*

---

# (i) information

---

## Contact details

Theatre Royal
18 Suffolk Street
London, SW1Y 4HT

☎ 0845 481 1870 (UK)
+44 (0)20 7930 8800 (non UK)

## Theatre Royal site

www.trh.co.uk

info@trh.co.uk

## Transport links

Piccadilly Circus

## 18

# THE NELL GWYNNE
### BULL INN COURT, WC2

See map p.9

##  THE PHANTOM LANDLORD

This tiny, dark, and atmospheric pub is tucked down a narrow alley leading off the Strand. Several customers have commented on feeling a strange coldness that seems to hang in the air to the left of the bar.

In 1997, the landlord became most perturbed by the frequency with which a ghostly hand patted him on his back pants pocket whenever he stood by this section of the counter.

Determined to discover the invisible revenant's identity, he paid a visit to a medium. The woman had no notion of what business the landlord was in, or even where he lived, but she informed him that she could sense an old man in a cloth cap, who had previously owned his property, and was very pleased with the way he was treating it.

She said that should this former resident ever be unhappy about the running of the building, he would stop at nothing to drive away those whom he held responsible. Interestingly, during the past decade, several landlords of The Nell Gwynne have attempted to alter the pub's appearance, and all have ended up leaving for unspecified reasons!

## (i) information

### Contact details

The Nell Gwynne
2 Bull Inn Court
London, WC2R 0NP

 +44 (0)20 7240 5579

 Pub guide site
www.beerintheevening.com
/pubs/s/42/421

### Transport links
Covent Garden;
Charing Cross;
Leicester Square

# ADELPHI THEATRE
STRAND, WC2

##  THE MURDERED ACTOR

On December 16, 1897, the actor and manager William Terris (see page 13) arrived at the stage door of the Adelphi Theatre in Maiden Lane for his evening performance in the play *Secret Service*. As he was unlocking the door, Richard Prince, a bit-part player, who had become jealous of the actor's success, rushed from the shadows and stabbed him. A crowd soon gathered around the dying man, who lay in the arms of his leading lady, Jessica Milward. As he slipped into unconsciousness, Terris whispered his barely audible last words: "I will be back."

In 1928, a tourist walking along Maiden Lane encountered a figure dressed in "old-fashioned, turn-of-the-century clothes" who suddenly vanished into thin air, "like a bubble bursting." Later, when shown a picture of William Terris, the tourist immediately recognized him as the man he had seen.

One afternoon in the same year, an actress was resting between performances in her dressing room at the Adelphi, when she was suddenly gripped by the arms— the chaise lounge on which she lay began to lurch violently from side to side.

A green light appeared over her dressing-room mirror and she heard two loud raps, emanating from behind the glass, and all went quiet. She later discovered that her dressing room was the one that Jessica Milward used to occupy, and that, whenever he passed it, Terris was in the habit of always knocking twice upon her door.

##  information

### Contact details
Adelphi Theatre
Strand
London, WC2

 0844 412 4651 (UK)

### Theatre guide site
www.londontheatre.co.uk
/londontheatre/westend
venues/adelphi.htm

### Transport links
Covent Garden;
Charing Cross;
Leicester Square

**20**

# LANGHAM HILTON HOTEL
PORTLAND PLACE, W1

See map p.9

## 👉 THE THING IN ROOM 333

A forerunner of London's grand hotels, the Langham Hotel was built in 1864. Its splendor was host to such famous names as Napoleon III of France and the composer Dvorák—who managed to offend the sensibilities of the management when, in an attempt to save money, he requested a double room for himself and his grown-up daughter.

But as even grander hotels were built across London, the Langham's popularity waned and by the 1950s it had been pressed into service as administrative offices for the British Broadcasting Corporation (BBC), which still has radio studios opposite the hotel. Several rooms on the fourth floor were maintained as accommodation for staff whose early starts or late finishes necessitated an overnight stay.

One night in 1973, announcer James Alexander Gordon was sleeping in Room 333 when he awoke to find a fluorescent ball hovering on the opposite side of the room. As he watched, it began to take on the clearly defined form of an Edwardian gentleman in full evening dress. Summoning up all his courage, the terrified presenter

asked who the apparition was and what it wanted. The question seemed to irritate the phantom, for it began to come toward him, its arms outstretched and eyes fixed and unblinking. Unable to take any more, Gordon rushed from the room and raced down to the doorman, who was not in the least bit sympathetic and refused point blank to accompany him back to the room. Gordon returned to Room 333 alone and found his mysterious guest still present, although its appearance seemed less distinct than it had been. When he told his colleagues about his ordeal, others told of encountering the apparition in that same bedroom.

The building has now been completely renovated and once more functions as a luxury hotel. However, ghostly activity continues in Room 333. In May 2003, a woman staying in the room checked out of the hotel suddenly, without giving any reason for her premature departure. A few days later, she sent a letter explaining that her slumber had been interrupted by the activities of the ghost that kept her awake by repeatedly shaking the bed during the night.

 *The resident wraith in Room 333 still troubles guests at the hotel.*

---

# (i) information

---

## Contact details

Langham Hilton Hotel
1c Portland Place
Regent Street
London, W1B 1JA

 +44 (0)20 7636 1000

**Langham site**

london.langhamhotels.co.uk

info@langhamhotels.com

## Transport links

⊖ Oxford Circus

# COUTTS BANK
STRAND, WC2 See map p.9

##  TROUBLE AT THE BANK

In November 1993, the directors of Coutts Bank took the unusual step of calling upon the services of the psychic medium Eddie Burks, in the hope that he would be able to lay to rest the phantom in the bank's computer room. A bank spokesperson told *The Times* how some staff had reported "lights going on and off ... and an apparition, a shadow was how it was described."

A séance was duly held in the course of which Burks made contact with the spirit and learned that it was Thomas Howard, 4th Duke of Norfolk. Howard's plot to marry Mary, Queen of Scots, and depose Mary's cousin Elizabeth I in her favor, had resulted in his execution.

"I was beheaded on a summer's day," the dejected duke informed Burks, "I have held much bitterness and ... I must let this go. In the name of God I ask your help ... "

On November 15, 1993, a congregation that included the present Duke and Duchess of Norfolk gathered at a nearby Catholic church to say prayers for Thomas Howard's soul. On leaving the service, the duke was asked if he was glad that his ancestor was finally at rest. "Actually," came the reply, "I don't believe in ghosts."

---

##  information

### Contact details
Coutts Bank
440 Strand
London, WC2R 0QS

☎ +44 (0)20 7753 1000

🖥 **London guide site**
www.allinlondon.co.uk
/directory/1063/11737.php

### Transport links
⊖ Charing Cross;
Leicester Square;
Embankment

# DUKE OF YORK'S THEATRE

**ST MARTIN'S LANE, WC2**

See map p.9 (10)

`23`

## ☞ THE STRANGLER JACKET

Designed in 1892 by British architect Walter Emden for Frank Wyatt and his wife, Violet Melnotte, the Duke of York's Theatre was the first theater to be built on St Martin's Lane. Violet managed the theater between 1923 and 1928, but she has shown a marked reluctance to leave. Her ghost has frequently been seen on opening nights.

A disturbing series of events at the theater in the late 1940s have become legendary in both theatrical and paranormal circles. Among the costumes worn in the production *The Queen Came By* was an old bolero-style jacket that acquired a sinister reputation for attempting to strangle any actress who wore it.

In an attempt to solve the mystery of what lay behind the phenomenon, a séance was held and one of the mediums clearly saw a man attempting to drown a struggling young woman. Eventually the victim's body collapsed, limp and lifeless, and the man proceeded to remove her clothing, including the bolero-style jacket. He then wrapped her corpse in a blanket and carried it away.

With such a heritage, the garment was considered an unsuitable prop and was sold on to an American collector of Victoriana. When his wife tried on the jacket, she too experienced the uncomfortable sensation of strangulation. Its current whereabouts are unknown.

## ⓘ information

### Contact details

Duke of York's Theatre
St Martin's Lane
London
WC2N 4BG

 **Duke of York's Theatre site**
www.dukeofyorkstheatre.co.uk

☎ 0844 871 7627 (UK)

### Transport links

⊖ Covent Garden;
Charing Cross;
Leicester Square

# HANDEL HOUSE MUSEUM

BROOK STREET, W1         See map p.9 (11)

##  THE FEMALE SPIRIT THAT CAME TO STAY

George Frideric Handel lived at 25 Brook Street for 36 years and died in the upstairs bedroom in 1759. In 2000, the upper stories of the building were leased to the Handel House Trust and on November 8, 2001 the Handel House Museum was opened to the public.

During the restoration project, it became apparent that the building was haunted and in July 2001 the Handel House Trust went as far as to call upon the services of a local priest to see if he could lay the ghost to rest. "We weren't sure whether having a ghost would attract or deter customers," commented Martin Egglestone, a trust fundraiser, who twice encountered the apparition in the room where Handel died. He described the apparition as female and observed that "there was no malevolent feeling. It felt like the pressure you get when you brush past someone in the Tube."

Staff also reported a strong scent of perfume hanging in the air of the bedroom. Although Handel lived here alone, he was visited by two sopranos, Faustina Bordoni and Francesca Cuzzoni. The two singers vied with each other to perform in the composer's operas and it's possible the ghost might be that of one of them.

◀ *A ghostly presence can be felt at Handel's former residence.*

## (i) information

### Contact details

Handel House Museum
25 Brook Street
Mayfair
London, W1K 4HB

 +44 (0)20 7495 1685

 **Handel House Museum site**
www.handelhouse.org

mail@handelhouse.org

### Transport links

⊖ Bond Street

# 26

# JOHN SNOW
## BROADWICK STREET, W1

See map p.9

## ☞ THE PHANTOM WITH THE BLOOD-RED EYES

The John Snow public house is named after John Snow, the doctor who saved the lives of thousands of Londoners in the early 19th century by proving that cholera was a waterborne disease. Quite who haunts the pub is not known, but several managers have reported feeling an invisible, icy presence brushing past them as they count the takings at the end of the day.

Some customers have also recounted spotting a shadowy figure sitting in the corner of the bar, its face twisted into a pain-racked grimace and its ghastly red eyes staring into space. It has been speculated that it might be the ghost of one of the unfortunate victims of the cholera epidemic, which devastated Soho in 1854.

▲ *The twisted grimace of the ghost at the John Snow pub may well be that of a cholera victim.*

---

## ⓘ information

**Contact details**

John Snow
39 Broadwick Street
London, W1F 9QP

 +44 (0)20 7437 1344

 **Pub guide site**
www.beerintheevening.com
/pubs/s/30/3096
/John_Snow/Soho

**Transport links**

 Oxford Cricus;
Piccadilly Circus;
Tottenham Court Road

# LONDON PALLADIUM
## ARGYLL STREET, W1

##  THE SPECTRAL LADY IN THE CRINOLINE DRESS

Opened in 1910 as the Palladium Music Hall, this luxurious theater became the London Palladium in 1934.

It was during a television interview in March 1973 that a doorman gave the first hint of something otherworldly roaming the theater.

The building's ghostly presence has a penchant for the Old Crimson Staircase located at the rear of the Royal Circle and which is believed to be a remnant of Argyll House, which stood on the site until 1864.

A spectral lady in a crinoline dress has been seen gliding up and down the staircase by a number of people, including usherettes, theater hands, and visiting artistes. Nobody knows who the woman is, although it has been suggested that she might be Mrs. Shireburn, mistress of the Duke of Argyll —who lived in Argyll House between 1750 and 1762— and to whom the duke left his entire property in England.

---

## (i) information

### Contact details

London Palladium
Argyll Street
London, W1F 7TF

 0844 412 2704 (UK)

 Theater guide site
www.londontheatredirect.com/venue/4/London-Palladium.aspx

### Transport links

 Oxford Circus

**28**

# THE CLERMONT CLUB
## BERKELEY SQUARE, W1

See map p.9

##  THE SPECTRAL SERVANT

The writer and historian Nikolaus Pevsner described 44 Berkeley Square as "the finest terrace house of London"; while the writer Horace Walpole applauded the building's staircase as being "... as beautiful a piece of scenery and, considering the space, of art as can be imagined ..."

The house was designed in 1742 by William Kent for Lady Isabella Finch, a maid of honor to George II's sister, Princess Amelia. Behind its elegant Palladian façade, Lady Isabella entertained many luminaries of her age, the proceedings and servants being watched over by her devoted major-domo, who cut a dashing figure in his green livery and powdered wig.

Lord Clermont subsequently bought the house and frequently entertained the Prince Regent, the future George IV, here. Having passed through a succession of owners, in 1959 the Clermont Club took over occupancy, but Lady Isabella's major-domo has chosen to linger on.

Over the last two centuries, his ghost has often been seen on the Grand Staircase, keeping a watchful eye on the playing of roulette and backgammon, which now goes on in the Grand Salon. After a fleeting appearance, he melts through one of the staircase doors and ascends the spiral staircase to his former bedroom at the top of the house.

*The spirit of Lady Isabella's major-domo lingers on at the Clermont Club.*

---

##  information

### Contact details

The Clermont Club
44 Berkeley Square
Mayfair, London, W1J 5AR

 +44 (0)20 7493 5587

 The Clermont Club site
www.theclermontclub.com

### Transport links

Green Park

# BURLINGTON ARCADE

MAYFAIR, W1
See map p.9  **15**

##  PERCY THE POLTERGEIST

British architect Samuel Ware designed Burlington Arcade for Lord George Cavendish in 1819, reputedly to prevent passers-by throwing oyster shells and other trash over the wall of his lordship's home next door, Burlington House. The arcade is still patrolled by top-hatted attendants, whose job it is to enforce Regency laws that forbid shoppers to sing, whistle, or hurry.

In the 1970s, a leather-goods store in the arcade was plagued by the nocturnal activities of a poltergeist that staff came to know as "Percy." It would seem that objects were lifted off the shelves in the middle of the night to be found the next morning arranged in neat semicircles upon the floor.

Scotland Yard detectives, having eliminated the possibility of human involvement, found themselves at a loss to explain the phenomena. Meanwhile, the management of the store, spotting the opportunity to enjoy some amusing publicity, placed a sign in the window announcing: "Poltergeists Gladly Served without Fear or Favour." This seemed to curb Percy's appetite for mayhem, and shortly afterward his disturbances ceased and have not been repeated since.

---

## (i) information

### Contact details

Burlington Arcade
Mayfair
London, W1

 **Burlington Arcade site**
www.burlington-arcade.co.uk

### Transport links

⊖ Piccadilly Circus;
Green Park

# FORTNUM AND MASON

PICCADILLY, W1

See map p.9 **(16)**

##  THE FARE-DODGING SPECTER OF LADY C

Founded in 1707, this upmarket store on Piccadilly supplies provisions to the Royal Household.

In the early 1960s, broadcaster and journalist Nancy Spain was standing outside the main entrance of Fortnum and Mason, attempting to hail a taxi to take her to an important appointment. Every cab that drove by was occupied and she became concerned that she would be late for her meeting. However, a taxi finally stopped alongside her, and a red-haired old woman climbed out and proceeded to search frantically in her purse for the fare. Desperate to be on her way, Nancy eventually stepped forward and paid for the old lady herself. Thanking Nancy for her kindness, the woman hurried into the store. As Nancy settled back into the cab en route to her appointment, the driver could not conceal his mirth. "You was caught there luv," he told her. "That was old Lady C. She hates paying her own fare, but she could buy and sell both of us."

As it happened Nancy Spain was quite amused by the incident. The next day she went to visit her mother, whom she told of her encounter with the miserly aristocrat. Nancy's mother looked surprised, but remained strangely silent. Rising from her chair, she picked up a newspaper dated three days earlier and passed it to Nancy. Open-mouthed, she read the headline: "LADY C DIES IN A FIRE."

##  information

### Contact details

Fortnum and Mason
181 Piccadilly
London, W1A 1ER

 +44 (0)20 7734 8040

 **Fortum and Mason site**
www.fortnumandmason.com

### Transport links

 Piccadilly Circus;
Green Park

**32**

# 50 BERKELEY SQUARE
## MAYFAIR, W1

See map p.9

##  THE MOST HAUNTED HOUSE IN LONDON

Charles Harper in *Haunted Houses* (1907) stated that "… it seems that a Something or Other, very terrible indeed, haunts or did haunt a particular room. This unnamed Raw Head and Bloody Bones, or whatever it is, has been sufficiently awful to have caused the death, in convulsions, of at least two foolhardy persons who have dared to sleep in that chamber … "

One of these persons was a nobleman who scoffed at tales that a hideous entity was residing within the haunted room and vowed to spend the night there. It was agreed, however, that he would ring the servants' bell to summon his friends if he required assistance. A little after midnight there was a faint ring, which was followed by a ferocious pealing of the bell. Rushing upstairs, the friends threw open the door and found their companion rigid with terror, his eyes bulging from their sockets. He was unable to tell them what he had seen, and such was the shock to his system that he died shortly afterward.

Many theories have been put forward to account for the haunting of 50 Berkeley Square. Harper reported that the house had once belonged to a Mr. Du Préco of Wilton Park, who locked his lunatic brother in one of the attics. The captive was so violent that he could only be fed through a hole in the door, and his groans and cries could be heard in the neighboring houses. It's possible that in death the madman refused to leave his past home.

*Although ghosts still wander the interior of 50 Berkeley Square, they are nowhere near as malevolent*
*as they were in the late 19th century when their antics gave the building a truly sinister reputation.*

##  information

### Contact details

Mayfair
50 Berkeley Square
London, W1J 5BA

[www] **Author site**
www.haunted-london.com
/50-berkeley-square

### Transport links

Green Park;
Bond Street

# CLERKENWELL TO EMBANKMENT

For centuries Clerkenwell, sitting on the banks of the underground river Fleet, included London's most infamous ghettos and was a place to be avoided. Today, straying into the back streets of Holborn brings you into some wonderfully atmospheric places, like Lincoln's Inn Fields, where the ghostly vestiges of past executions drift on the night breezes. By contrast, Temple is a gas-lit oasis from which many former residents are loath to depart.

## HAUNTED LOCATIONS

( 1 ) Red Lion Square

( 2 ) The Ship Tavern

( 3 ) Charles Dickens Museum

( 4 ) The Dolphin Tavern

( 5 ) Lincoln's Inn Fields

( 6 ) Ye Olde Cock Tavern

( 7 ) The George

( 8 ) Aldwych Station

( 9 ) Sadler's Wells Theatre

( 10 ) The Temple

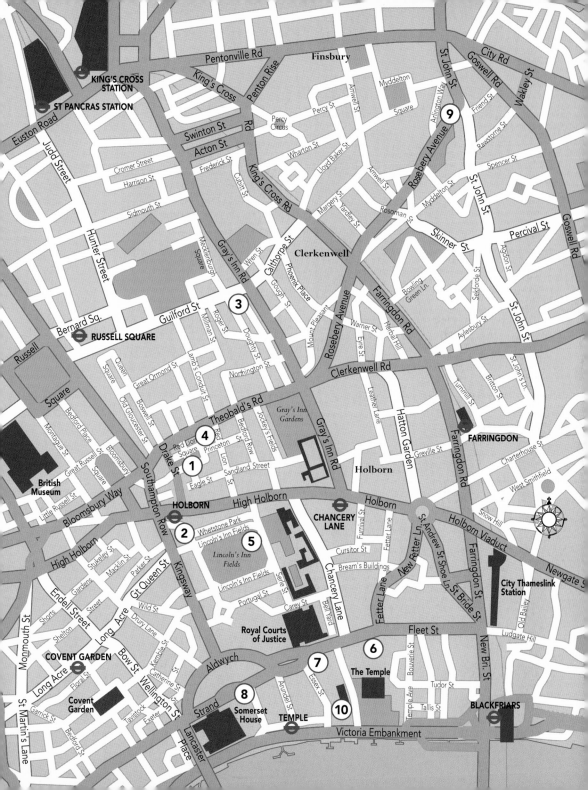

# 36 RED LION SQUARE
## CAMDEN, WC1

See map p.35 (1)

 ## THE GHOSTLY REGICIDES

The huge trees that tower over the center of Red Lion Square cast it into almost perpetual shadow, and it comes as no surprise to learn that the place is haunted.

In 1660, Charles II returned from exile in the Netherlands and the Restoration of the monarchy began after the Commonwealth under Oliver Cromwell. Those who had remained loyal to the Royalist cause could look forward to rewards, while those who had supported the Parliamentarian campaign and had welcomed the rule of Cromwell could expect retribution now that a Stuart sat upon the throne of England again.

The three leading Parliamentarians Oliver Cromwell, John Bradshaw, and Henry Ireton were beyond the king's reach —they lay buried in the hallowed earth of

Westminster Abbey. Unwilling to let a little thing like death stand in his way, the king demanded vengeance and, on January 29, 1661, the cadavers of the three men were exhumed and put on trial for regicide.

Though the men had cheated the ax in life, they would not do so in death. Found guilty, they were sentenced to beheading at Tyburn.

The bodies of Cromwell and Ireton were brought to the Red Lion Inn, which then stood on the site of Red Lion Square. They remained there overnight, and at dawn the next day, they were taken to Tyburn, where along with the putrefied corpse of Bradshaw they were hanged by their necks

 *Henry Ireton, along with Oliver Cromwell and John Bradshaw, undertakes nocturnal spectral rambles across Red Lion Square.*

until late afternoon. Once cut down, their heads were hacked off and placed on spikes above Westminster Hall, while their bodies were buried in a deep pit beneath the gallows.

Since then, their ghosts have returned to haunt Red Lion Square on many occasions. The three men, complete in body, appear to be involved in a deep and animated conversation as they stroll purposefully across the square. Once they come to the middle of the square, their revenants become blurry and, with each ghostly step thereafter, they become more and more indistinct—until they melt away.

---

 ## information

### Contact details

Red Lion Square
Camden
London, WC1

Camden Council site
www.camden.gov.uk/ccm/content
/leisure/outdoor-camden/parks
/great-parks-in-camden.en?page=13

### Transport links

⊖ Holborn

**38**

# THE SHIP TAVERN
## GATE STREET, WC2

See map p.35

 ## THE FUGITIVES' HIDEAWAY

During the despotic reign of Tudor king Henry VIII, who imposed Protestantism on England, Catholics would sneak to the building that once stood on the site that is now occupied by this cozy 18th-century hostelry to attend mass, conducted by then-outlawed priests. Lookouts would give a prearranged signal, warning the congregation when the king's zealous officials came into view. The signal would, hopefully, give the priest enough time to escape into one of the pub's several "hidey-holes," and allow the congregation time to take up their tankards and become just another group of regulars.

Listening as the king's officers searched for them and knowing that discovery would mean imprisonment, torture, and certain death, those brave priests must have been quaking with fear. The feeling of relief when the officials had departed must have been immense.

It is this aura of relief that often pervades the atmosphere of the pub, and the staff are extremely fond of their "happy" ghost. He never actually shows himself, but he makes his presence known with his mischievous pranks, such as hiding cooking utensils for several days or moving cellar keys to other parts of the pub.

*Enjoy the hospitality of The Ship Tavern and you well may encounter the happy specter that roams the pub.*

---

##  information

### Contact details

The Ship Tavern
12 Gate Street
Holborn
London, WC2A 3HP

 +44 (0)20 7405 1992

The Ship Tavern site
www.theshiptavern.co.uk

info@theshiptavern.co.uk

### Transport links

Russell Square;
Holborn;
Chancery Lane

**40**

# CHARLES DICKENS MUSEUM
## DOUGHTY STREET, WC1

See map p.35 **3**

##  CHARLES DICKENS RETURNS

The old residence of writer Charles Dickens is a treasure trove of relics and articles that depict the great author's life and times. His ghost appears to relish the pull of the only one of his London homes to have survived and he has been seen on many occasions. One former curator claimed that she frequently saw Dickens's distinctive figure bounding enthusiastically along the hallway and up the staircase.

In 1972, a group of builders working on an adjacent property saw the great man glide past them on the sidewalk outside, drift up the steps, and promptly disappear into the solid front door. One of the workmen is said to have been so affected by the experience that he resigned on the spot.

 *Dickens wrote some of his greatest works, such as* Oliver Twist, *while living at Doughty Street.*

---

## (i) information

### Contact details

Charles Dickens Museum
48 Doughty Street
London, WC1N 2LX

☎ +44 (0)20 7405 2127

Charles Dickens Museum site
www.dickensmuseum.com

### Transport links

Russell Square

# THE DOLPHIN TAVERN

RED LION STREET, WC1      See map p.35 (4)

##  WHEN DEATH RAINED DOWN

The Dolphin Tavern is very much a locals' pub and boasts an interior that is functional rather than fashionable. On one of its walls you can see a battered old clock, the hands of which are frozen at 10:40 pm, much as they have been for almost 90 years. It was at this precise moment on September 9, 1915 that a Zeppelin bomb crashed onto the pub and reduced it to a smoldering heap of twisted rubble. Three customers were killed and several others were seriously injured in the tragedy.

The clock was dragged from the ruins, and when the pub was rebuilt, it was placed on the wall as a permanent memorial to that night when death and destruction rained down from above. And, every so often, as the staff are tidying up after another day's trading, their attention is drawn to the clock. As they gaze upon its face, they hear a ghostly, mournful whistling that grows lower and lower, until all is quiet once more.

## (i) information

### Contact details

The Dolphin Tavern
44 Red Lion Street
Bloomsbury
London, WC1R 4PF

 +44 (0)20 7831 6298

 **Pub guide site**

www.beerintheevening.com
/pubs/s/10/1091
/Dolphin_Tavern/Bloomsbury

### Transport links

⊖ Holborn

**42**

# LINCOLN'S INN FIELDS
## CAMDEN, WC2
See map p.35 **5**

## ☞ THE GHOSTLY SCREAMS THAT NEVER DIE

There was a time when Lincoln's Inn Fields was used as a place of public execution. In 1586, Anthony Babington and his 13 coconspirators in a plot to assassinate Elizabeth I and put Mary, Queen of Scots, onto the throne were over two days hanged, drawn, and quartered in the fields. Babington was still conscious when he was eviscerated, and must have endured unimaginable agonies. After the queen heard of his suffering she decided on leniency and the remaining conspirators were shown the mercy of being hanged until dead before disembowelling commenced.

Another to be executed here was William, Lord Russell, who was sentenced to death in 1683 for plotting to kill Charles II. Lord Russell strolled bravely to his death, maintaining that the pain would last for but a moment and cause "less pain than the drawing of a tooth."

Unfortunately, the notorious, bungling Jack Ketch was wielding the ax and, according to the diarist John Evelyn, it "took three butcherly strokes" to remove his head. Ketch later defended his ineptitude with the claim, "His lordship moved!" With such a brutal and barbaric past, it is hardly surprising that ghosts aplenty are said to wander Lincoln's Inn Fields during the hours of darkness.

Lincoln's Inn Fields is also home to one of London's four Inns of Court—Lincoln's Inn. In the 18th century, Robert Perceval—cousin of Spencer Perceval (1762–1812), the only British Prime Minister ever to have been assassinated—came to read law here. However, he neglected his studies in favor of more hedonistic pursuits and fell into a thoroughly dissolute lifestyle.

One night, however, he took a break from his usual nocturnal activities of drinking, gambling, and whoring, and was studying in his chamber. As midnight approached, he started to grow a trifle uneasy. A cold shiver suddenly ran down his spine and, turning from his books, he saw a shrouded figure standing behind him. Leaping to his feet, Perceval drew his sword and lurched at his mysterious visitor only to be astonished when the blade passed through it. Dropping his weapon, he pulled

 *Ghostly moans have been known to shatter the stillness of Lincoln's Inn Fields in the dead of night.*

the shroud away from the specter's face and found himself face to face with his own image—but with gaping wounds to the face and chest.

Taking this as a warning that he must mend his ways, Perceval became a reformed character, but this change was predictably short lived. One morning, his corpse was found sprawled in a gutter on the Strand. He had been run through with his own sword, and his horrific injuries mirrored those he had seen upon the apparition.

---

# ⓘ information

---

## Contact details

Lincoln's Inn Fields
Camden
London, WC2A

🖥 **London guide site**
www.londontown.com/LondonStreets
/lincolns_inn_fields_1f3.html

## Transport links

⊖ Holborn;
Chancery Lane

**44**

# YE OLDE COCK TAVERN
## FLEET STREET, EC4
See map p.35

##  OLIVER GOLDSMITH'S MACABRE MEANDERINGS

Dating back to the mid-16th century, Ye Olde Cock Tavern is Fleet Street's oldest pub. It stood on the opposite side of the road originally, but moved to its current location in the early 19th century.

Past patrons have included Samuel Pepys and the poet Alfred, Lord Tennyson, who once composed a poem to the pub's head waiter. The pub is believed to be haunted by the writer Oliver Goldsmith, who is buried in Temple Churchyard to the rear of the establishment.

One night in September 1984, an Australian barmaid was given the task of taking out the trash, which was left for collection behind the building.

Opening the door she found herself face to face with the disembodied head of a man, which was floating in mid-air before her. Letting out an almighty scream, she raced back inside where landlady Sarah Kennedy calmed her down with a stiff brandy.

Having regained her composure, the girl agreed that it might be best if she went upstairs for a rest. But no sooner had she got to the second floor landing, than she began screaming again. Her colleagues rushed to assist and found her looking aghast at a picture of Oliver Goldsmith that was hanging on the wall. "That's him!" she cried, "That's the face I saw!"

##  information

### Contact details

Ye Olde Cock Tavern
22 Fleet Street
London, EC4Y 1AA

☎ +44 (0)20 7353 8570

[www] Pub guide site
www.beerintheevening.com/pubs/s/25/2516/Ye_Olde_Cock_Tavern/Fleet_Street

### Transport links

 Temple; Chancery Lane; Blackfriars

# THE GEORGE
### STRAND, WC2

See map p.35 **7**

##  THE HANDSOME PHANTOM

Although the current black-and-white timbered frontage of The George pub dates from the 1930s, it stands on much older foundations and is the haunt of a ghost of 17th-century origin.

One morning during a refurbishment in the 1970s, a gang of painters and decorators began work at the pub. Having allotted various tasks to his men, the foreman went down into the old cellar and set about whitewashing its walls. After about 20 minutes, he came racing back upstairs. "That feller down there, gu'vnor," the terrified decorator panted to the landlord, "he just looked at me, didn't say nothin', just stared." The landlord calmed him down with a glass of brandy and then asked him what the man had looked like. "All 'istorical like them Roundheads and Cavaliers," came the breathless reply. The landlord nodded. "Oh I shouldn't worry about him," he reassured the workman. "That's just the ghost. My wife sees him all the time."

Quite who he is, or was, nobody has been able to ascertain, but there is a long tradition of this handsome phantom appearing to startled witnesses in the cellar of The George.

---

##  information

---

### Contact details

The George
213 Strand
London, WC2R 1AP

 +44 (0)20 7353 9638

 **The George site**
www.capitalpubcompany.com
/the-george

### Transport links

⊖ Temple

**46**

# ALDWYCH STATION
## STRAND, WC2
See map p.35

## ☞ THE GHOST LINE

Aldwych Station opened on November 30, 1907. It was initially called Strand Station, but was soon renamed because at that time Charing Cross station was also called Strand, causing much confusion!

The line was used to run a shuttle service back and forth to Holborn Underground station and ran for 87 years until it was closed due to declining passenger numbers. The last train carrying the general public departed from the station on the evening of September 30, 1994.

The station stands on the site of the Royal Strand Theatre, which was demolished in 1905. This may account for the ghostly actress who is often seen strolling along the tracks at night. Indeed, the "fluffers"—those whose job it is to clean the underground's tunnels and stations at night—have often encountered this melancholic shade, and several of them have, reportedly, been absolutely terrified by the experience.

Today, the station is maintained by London Underground, primarily as a museum piece and film set, while the ticket hall is frequently rented out for art exhibitions, book launches, and other private parties. It is without doubt the most used of London Underground's abandoned stations and numerous films and television programs have been shot in its cavernous depths.

*A ghostly actress has been known to wander the underground tracks at night.*

## ⓘ information

### Contact details
Aldwych Station
Strand
London, WC2B

🖥 **London guide site**
www.underground-history.co.uk
/aldwych.php

### Transport links
🚇 Temple; Covent Garden

# SADLER'S WELLS THEATRE

ROSEBERY AVENUE, EC1                 See map p.35 ⑨

##  THE FEARS OF A CLOWN

The costly rebuilding of Sadler's Wells Theatre in the late 1990s belies the fact that it is one of London's oldest theater sites, founded in 1683 by Richard Sadler.

In April 1781, Joseph Grimaldi (see page 10) made his stage debut at the theater when he was just three years old. He went on to enjoy a successful theatrical career, during which he almost single-handedly laid the foundations for the modern pantomime tradition.

Grimaldi is best remembered as the creator of Joey the Clown, complete with whitened face and red half-moons on either cheek. He made his final stage appearance on March 17, 1828.

Grimaldi's macabre last request that his head should be severed from his body prior to burial was apparently carried out. This might account for the chilling apparition that was frequently seen at the theater prior to its rebuilding.

His disembodied head, recognizable by its white-painted face and glassy eyes, was seen several times, floating behind the occupants in one of the old boxes. Intriguingly, the people occupying the box never had any idea that they had been honored by an appearance until it was mentioned to them after the play! As yet, there have been no reports of similar hauntings in the new theater.

---

## ⓘ information

### Contact details

Sadler's Wells Theatre
Rosebery Avenue
London, EC1R 4TN

 0844 412 4300 (UK)
+44 (0)20 7863 8198 (non UK)

 **Saddler's Wells site**
www.sadlerswells.com

reception@sadlerswells.com

### Transport links

 Angel

## 50

# THE TEMPLE
TEMPLE PLACE, WC2

See map p.35

##  THE JUDGE GOES BY

The quiet, cloisterlike Middle and Inner Temples comprise two of London's four Inns of Court, which are set among the timeless alleyways and courtyards in which barristers have their chambers. It is a tranquil area that time and progress have left untouched, and its enchantment is at its most magical on dark winter nights, when the flickering glow of gaslight casts eerie shadows upon buildings that seem almost marooned in a bygone age. It is on such nights that the Temple's resident wraith stirs from his otherworldly slumber and hurries once more through places he knew well in life.

Henry Hawkins was one of the 19th century's most respected advocates. He was called to the bar in 1843 at the age of 26 and spent the rest of his illustrious career in and around the Temple.

So attached was Hawkins to the machinations and traditions of his chosen profession that his ghost has proved unwilling to depart from the gas-lit oasis where he made his name. He appears in the hours after midnight, wigged and robed and with a mass of dusty legal papers clutched in his arms. Witnesses can only look on as his shimmering figure races past them at a brisk pace. And as he does so, his image begins to fade until, after just a few tantalizing moments he dissolves into the night and returns to the realm whence he came.

*The ghost of Henry Hawkins seems intent on remaining at the Temple.* ▶

---

##  information

---

### Contact details
Temple
Temple Place
London, WC2R 2PH

### Transport links
⊖ Temple

# THE CITY & THE EAST END

This area of London is steeped in history and ghosts: from the spectral cries that echo over Smithfield Market to the shadowy monk who keeps a lone vigil inside London's oldest parish church, St Bartholomew the Great. We also stray into the gas-lit streets of the Victorian metropolis to ponder the infamous murders of Jack the Ripper. Pride of place belongs to the Tower of London, which holds the dubious distinction of being the most haunted building in the whole of England!

## HAUNTED LOCATIONS

1. St Paul's Cathedral
2. Amen Court
3. St Andrew's by the Wardrobe
4. West Smithfield
5. The Viaduct Tavern
6. 33 Cock Lane
7. St Bartholomew's Hospital
8. Ye Olde Red Cow
9. St Bartholomew the Great
10. Bunhill Fields
11. St James Garlickhythe
12. London Bridge
13. Tower of London
14. All Hallows by the Tower
15. Bank Underground Station
16. Bank of England
17. St Botolph's Church

# ST PAUL'S CATHEDRAL
## ST PAUL'S CHURCHYARD, EC4

See map p.53 (1)

### ☞ WHISTLER'S SECRET DOORWAY

Lord Horatio Herbert Kitchener's death, on June 3, 1916 was treated as a national calamity and there is a fitting memorial to him in St Paul's Cathedral. The Kitchener Chapel is adorned with an assortment of battle colors and a white marble effigy of the Secretary of War reclines on its floor.

If, as you stand gazing upon his memorial, a sudden chill passes over you, take note, for this is often the first hint that the cathedral's ghostly resident, "Whistler," is about to put in an appearance. Next, you will hear the low, barely audible sound of mournful whistling. Gazing into the chapel you may spy a wizened, old clergyman dressed in old-fashioned robes with flowing locks of gray hair. His tuneless whistling will grow steadily louder as he glides across the chapel and melts away slowly into the wall to the right of the gates.

Intriguingly, during the renovation work following World War I, when it was decided that the chapel should be re-dedicated to Lord Kitchener, workmen uncovered a hidden door behind the exact section of wall where the ghost always disappears. It opened onto a narrow, winding staircase that led up to a secret room within the inner fabric of the cathedral. Nobody had known of its existence, with, of course, the exception of the ghost, whomever he may have been.

*If you visit the Kitchener memorial, listen out for the cathedral's ghostly resident "Whistler."* ▶

## ⓘ information

### Contact details

St Paul's Cathedral
St Paul's Churchyard
London, EC4M 8AD

 +44 (0)20 7246 8357

 **St Paul's Cathedral site**
www.stpauls.co.uk

### Transport links

 St Paul's; Mansion House

 City Thameslink

## 56 | AMEN COURT
### WARWICK LANE, EC4

See map p.53 ②

##  THE REALM OF THE BLACK DOG

Amen Court is a delightful, hidden enclave of 17th- to 19th-century houses, where the Dean and Chapter of St Paul's Cathedral live. Famous past residents have included wit and author Sydney Smith, who lived at Number One between 1831 and 1834; and R. H. Barnham, author of the evocative and eerie *Ingoldsby Legends*, who occupied the same address from 1839 to 1845.

At the rear of the court, a large and ominous dark wall looms. Behind it once stood the fearsome bulk of Newgate Prison,

▼ Amen Court is haunted by the shuffling figure of a shapeless, black form known as the "Black Dog of Newgate," which is said to date from the 13th century.

which was demolished in 1902. However, there remains a tiny passage, which was known as "Deadman's Walk." The passage took its name from the fact that prisoners were led along it to their executions, and were buried beneath it afterward.

Although many ghostly tales have evolved around this sinister old wall, the most chilling is that of the "Black Dog of Newgate." This shapeless, black form slithers along the top of the wall, slides down into the courtyard and then melts away. Its manifestations are always accompanied by a nauseous smell and sometimes also by the sound of dragging footsteps. Its origins are said to date back to the reign of Henry III in the 13th century, when a fearsome famine struck London and the poor felons incarcerated within Newgate, faced with the prospect of starvation, turned to cannibalism as a means of survival. One day, a scholar was imprisoned there on charges of sorcery.

His portly figure proved too much of a temptation for the emaciated inmates and, within a few days, they killed and devoured him, pronouncing him to be "good meate."

However, the prisoners soon had cause to regret their actions, for a hideous black dog, with eyes of fire and jowls that dripped with blood, appeared in the dead of night and proceeded to exact a terrifying revenge, tearing the hapless prisoners limb from limb. Only when the murder of its master— the dead sorcerer—had been fully avenged, did the dog return to the prison's fetid dungeons, where it became a harbinger of death, appearing on the eve of executions or on the night before a felon breathed his last. When the prison was demolished in 1902, it was hoped that the black dog would become a thing of the past. But it was not to be. For people who happened to glance at the dark wall when walking in Amen Court at night have occasionally reported seeing its black shape, shuffling across the wall.

## ⓘ information

### Contact details

Amen Court
Warwick Lane
City of London
London, EC4

### Transport links

 St Paul's

 City Thameslink

**58**

# ST ANDREW'S BY THE WARDROBE

## ST ANDREW'S HILL, EC4

See map p.53 ③

## ☞ ASK NOT "FOR WHOM THE BELL TOLLS"

The unusual name of this red-brick church, which was built by acclaimed architect Sir Christopher Wren in 1695, refers to its former proximity to the King's Wardrobe, a suite of buildings where robes of state and cloth for the royal household were stored. The buildings were destroyed during the Great Fire of London (1666), after which the Wardrobe was moved to Westminster.

In 1933, three bells from the parish church at Avenbury, Herefordshire, were rehung in the belfry of St Andrew's by the Wardrobe. One of them, known as Gabriel, had been cast in Worcester in the 15th century, and it was an established piece of Avenbury folklore that, whenever a vicar of the church died, this bell would always ring of its own accord to mourn his passing.

Barely a year after its arrival in London, local residents were woken in the early hours of one morning by the knell of a solitary bell, sounding from the tower of the church. When local police arrived to investigate they found the building was locked and a cursory search revealed no sign of a forced entry. The next morning, word arrived that the vicar at Avenbury had died shortly before the mysterious chime was heard.

---

## ⓘ information

---

### Contact details

St Andrew's by
  the Wardrobe
St Andrew's Hill
London, EC4V 5DE

 St Andrew's by the Wardrobe site
www.standrewbythewardrobe.net

 +44 (0)20 7329 3632

### Transport links

 St Paul's; Mansion House

 City Thameslink

# WEST SMITHFIELD

WEST SMITHFIELD, EC1

##  DEATH BY FIRE AND ITS GHOSTLY EFFECTS

The "Smoothfield," as Smithfield was originally known, was for many years one of London's many places of execution. In August 1305, Sir William Wallace—popularly known as Braveheart—was put to death here, and a gray granite plaque on the wall of nearby St Bartholomew's Hospital still commemorates the Scotsman's heroic exploits.

During the reign of Queen Mary I in the mid-16th century, more than 200 Protestants were put to death in England, and many of them were burned at Smithfield. "Bloody Mary," as she was known, was emphatic that green wood should not be used during executions, as its smoke was likely to suffocate the victims before they suffered the full agony of the flames. We can only guess at the terrible suffering endured by those who perished here, as Mary strove to undo the work of her Protestant father Henry VIII and her half-brother Edward VI. Her determination to bring Roman Catholicism back to the people of England using fire and the sword allowed no room for mercy.

For some of her victims, the torment appears to have proved eternal. Many people who work in the area in the early hours of the morning have often been disturbed by anguished and agonized screams that fill the air—and worse still, by the sickly smell of burning flesh that is carried upon the night breeze.

##  information

### Contact details

West Smithfield
London, EC1

 **London guide site**
www.londontown.com
/LondonStreets/west_smith
field_496.html

### Transport links

 Farringdon; Barbican

**60**

# THE VIADUCT TAVERN
## NEWGATE STREET, EC1

See map p.53 **5**

##  DOWN IN THE CELLAR

The Viaduct Tavern stands opposite the Central Criminal Courts, more popularly known as the Old Bailey, after the road on which they stand. The pub dates from 1875 and is the last example of a late Victorian gin palace left in the City of London. It is also prone to bouts of poltergeist activity.

The restless spirit that haunts The Viaduct Tavern has a propensity to haunt the pub's cellars and several members of staff have experienced its unwelcome attentions.

One Saturday morning in 1996, a manager was tidying the cellar, when the door suddenly slammed shut and the lights went out. Feeling his way to the door, he discovered that, no matter how hard he pushed, it would not open. His wife heard his cries for help and came downstairs to investigate. She found that the doors, which would not open from the inside, were unlocked and easily opened from the outside.

In May 1999, two electricians were working in one of the pub's upstairs rooms, when one of them felt a tap on the shoulder. Thinking it was his workmate, he turned around but found that he was on the other side of the room. He asked him if he was playing a prank, but the man denied any involvement. As he was about to return to his chores, both men watched as the heavy carpet, which lay rolled up by the window, was lifted into the air and then dropped.

*The Viaduct Tavern dates from 1875 and is haunted by a mischievous sprite called "Fred."*

## (i) information

### Contact details

The Viaduct Tavern
126 Newgate Street
London, EC1A 7AA

 +44 (0)20 7600 1863

### Pub guide site

www.beerintheevening.com
/pubs/s/54/5472/Viaduct_
Tavern/St_Pauls

### Transport links

St Pauls; Blackfriars; Farringdon

# 33 COCK LANE
## CITY OF LONDON, EC1

See map p.53

## ☞ SCRATCHING FANNY

Number 33 Cock Lane was demolished long ago, but in the late 18th century one of London's most infamous hauntings occurred at what was then the home of a clerk called William Parsons.

One morning in 1760, Parsons offered lodgings to a widower called William Kent.

He gratefully accepted and moved into the house with his sister-in-law, Miss Fanny, with whom he had become romantically involved.

Not long after the lovers had taken up residence, Parsons borrowed a large sum of money from Kent but showed a marked reluctance to repay it. Relations had become

▼ Cock Lane as it looked in the 18th century; contrasted with its appearance today.

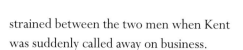
strained between the two men when Kent was suddenly called away on business.

Rather than sleep alone while her lover was away, Miss Fanny took Parsons's 11-year-old daughter, Elizabeth, to bed with her. In the early hours of the morning, they were woken by a mysterious scratching noise sounding from behind the wainscoting. Fanny convinced herself that it was the spirit of her dead sister, warning her of her own imminent demise. When Kent returned, he found his mistress on the verge of a nervous breakdown and he deemed it best that they move out of the lodgings. However, soon after they found a new home, Fanny died of smallpox and was buried in a vault at St John's Church, Clerkenwell.

When Kent pressed Parsons for repayment of the loan, his former landlord claimed that the scratching noises had resumed in his house and that they were the spirit of Miss Fanny and that she had informed him that William Kent had actually murdered her.

A local clergyman decided that an investigation into the allegations should be carried out and the ghost proved more than willing to oblige. The wraith informed him, through Parsons, that if he spent a night by Miss Fanny's resting place in St John's Church, then she would answer any questions by knocking on the lid of her coffin. And so it was that the vicar, accompanied by a group of fearless companions traipsed down into the church vault at 1 am one morning. When nothing had occurred by dawn, the ghost was declared a fraud.

However, a secret watch had been kept on Elizabeth, who was observed hiding a small wooden board beneath her stays, and the trick was exposed. Parsons spent two years in the King's Bench Prison. Elizabeth was exonerated of any crime as it was deemed that she had been an unwitting accomplice and William Kent's name was cleared. The ghost was consigned to the pages of history as "Scratching Fanny of Cock Lane!"

---

## ⓘ information

---

### Contact details

33 Cock Lane
City of London
London, EC1A

### Transport links

🚇 Farringdon; Barbican; St Paul's

 City Thameslink

**64**

# ST BARTHOLOMEW'S HOSPITAL
## WEST SMITHFIELD, EC1

See map p.53

##  THE COFFIN LIFT

St Bartholomew's, or Bart's as it is known to those who study and work there, has the distinction of being the oldest hospital in London to stand on its original site. Its origins stretch back to 1123, when it was founded as part of the monastery of St Bartholomew by Rahere, a court jester, turned man of God (see page 66).

In the depths of the hospital, there is an elevator, which generations of doctors and nurses have come to know as the "coffin lift." In the silent hours of early mornings, the elevator has been known to take bemused passengers down to the basement, irrespective of which floor they have requested. Once there, its lights go out. After a few moments of madly pushing its buttons, staff are able to open the gates and walk back up to the first floor. Here they find the elevator waiting, its gates open and its lights on. Should they then choose to walk up to the level they requested, they suffer the unnerving experience of having the elevator follow them up the shaft, around which the staircase twists. Tradition maintains that the ghost responsible for the malfunction is a nurse who was murdered in the elevator by a deranged patient.

---

## (i) information

### Contact details
St Bartholomew's
 Hospital
West Smithfield
London, EC1A 7BE

 +44 (0)20 7377 7000

www St Bartholomew's Hospital site
www.bartsandthelondon.nhs.uk

### Transport links
Barbican; Farringdon;
St Paul's

# YE OLDE RED COW

LONG LANE, EC1

See map p.53 **8**

##  DICK O'SHEA KEEPS A GHOSTLY WATCH

Ye Olde Red Cow is a snug little pub that stands opposite Europe's largest meat market, Smithfield Meat Market.

The butchers and meatpackers work throughout the night, and so many of the pubs in this area have special licenses that allow them to open between the hours of 6:30 am and 9 am. Ye Olde Red Cow is one of these market pubs, and for many years in the late 20th century, it was run by Dick O'Shea, a colorful Irishman who numbered among his clientele the actors Peter Ustinov and Bernard Miles. They, along with many others, were attracted by Dick's legendary hot whiskey toddies.

Ever the benign host once the pub opened, Dick sat in a favored rocking chair, rocking back and forth, as he kept a watchful eye on comings and goings.

He died in 1981, but his spirit apparently found it difficult to adjust. For almost a year after his demise, regulars caught frequent glimpses of his unmistakable form, sitting in his rocking chair, a warm smile upon his face, as genial and watchful a host in death as ever he had been in life.

---

##  information

### Contact details

Ye Olde Red Cow
71 Long Lane
Clerkenwell
London, EC1A 9EJ

 +44 (0)20 7726 2595

 **London guide site**
www.londontown.com/
LondonInformation/Bars_
and_Clubs/Ye_Olde_Red_
Cow/c206

### Transport links

⊖ Farringdon; Barbican

**66**

# ST BARTHOLOMEW THE GREAT
## KINGHORN STREET, EC1

See map p.53

##  FOOTSTEPS IN THE NIGHT

The Priory Church of St Bartholomew the Great is the oldest parish church in London. It was founded in 1123 by Rahere —a court jester turned monk who decided to make a pilgrimage to Rome.

During his trip, St Bartholomew appeared to him in a dream and urged him to found a church in his name, which he did on his return. Rahere's remains were buried within the church when he died in 1145.

His tomb now stands just to the left of the altar, its reverse side clearly showing the results of a hasty repair carried out in the 19th century when the parish officials decided to report upon the state of the founder's body. It was well preserved, and even Rahere's clothes and sandals are said to have been intact. A few days after the tomb was resealed, one of the church officers fell ill and confessed that, when the tomb had been open, he had stolen one of the sandals. He gave it back and recovered, but it was never returned to the foot of its rightful owner. Since that day, Rahere has haunted the church as a shadowy, hooded figure that appears from the gloom, brushes past astonished witnesses and fades slowly into thin air.

*A ghostly monk walks the "Holy Gloom" of St Bartholomew the Great, London's oldest parish church.* ▶

---

## (i) information

---

### Contact details

St Bartholomew the Great
6 Kinghorn Street
London, EC1A 7HW

 +44 (0)20 7606 5171

www St Bartholomew the Great site
www.greatstbarts.com

admin@greatstbarts.com

### Transport links

 Farringdon; Barbican; St Paul's

# 68 BUNHILL FIELDS
## CITY ROAD, EC1

See map p.53 **10**

## ☞ WHEN THE DEAD WALKED AGAIN

The name of this ancient city burial ground, which is crammed with an eclectic mix of tombs and gravestones, is probably derived from Bone Hill. Since there is no proof that the ground here was ever consecrated, it was a favored burial place

▼ *Several of the gardeners at Bunhill Fields have complained of supernatural activity.*

for nonconformists, who were able to bury their dead without the use of the Common Prayer Book. Writers John Bunyan, Daniel Defoe, and William Blake are just a few of those whose graves are shaded by soaring plane trees. The spiked gate at the graveyard's northeast corner was put up specially to deter the nefarious activities of the body snatchers, who were responsible for stealing corpses and selling them to medics for dissection.

Although no burials have taken place here since 1854, the Corporation of London still maintains the ground for public usage and employs several gardeners to ensure that this vast necropolis remains in pristine condition.

In June 2001, several of the gardeners complained of experiencing supernatural phenomena. "Things have gone a bit haywire in the last 10 months," one of them told the *Highbury and Islington Gazette*, "… loads of weird stuff has started happening." Steam was seen rising from graves; several gardeners spoke of encountering a cloaked woman who suddenly disappeared without a trace; while floods of water would suddenly appear from nowhere, even on dry days. Meanwhile, the gardeners' hut, which had long been considered a safe haven from whatever supernatural forces were loose in the fields, began to suffer the attentions of the ghostly residents.

Gardener Bill Underwood told how he had unlocked the door one morning, and discovered that "all our posters and notices had mysteriously been taken down and arranged neatly on the floor in exactly the same order." Strange handprints had also appeared on the table, which certainly did not belong to any of the staff. When he was asked if he had any idea who or what was responsible for the activity, Bill could only shrug his shoulders and express bemusement.

---

## (i) information

### Contact details

Bunhill Fields
38 City Road
London, EC1Y 2BG

 +44 (0)20 7247 8548

 **Independent guide site**
www.sacred-destinations.com/england/london-bunhill-fields

### Transport links

⊖ Old Street

**70**

# ST JAMES GARLICKHYTHE
## GARLICK HILL, EC4 See map p.53 **11**

###  JIMMY GARLICK, THE GHOSTLY MUMMY

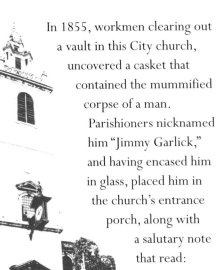

In 1855, workmen clearing out a vault in this City church, uncovered a casket that contained the mummified corpse of a man. Parishioners nicknamed him "Jimmy Garlick," and having encased him in glass, placed him in the church's entrance porch, along with a salutary note that read:

*Stop Stranger As You Pass By.
As You Are Now So Once Was I.*

*As I Am Now So Shall You Be.
So Pray Prepare To Follow Me.*

During World War II, a bomb dropped through the roof of the porch and, although it didn't explode, it landed uncomfortably close to the cabinet, shattering its glass. This appears to have stirred Jimmy's revenant to indignation, and his ghost has wandered the church ever since.

Jimmy's mortal remains are now kept away from public gaze in an upper room of the church tower. He is thought to have been 16-year-old Seagrave Chamberlain, who died from a fever on December 17, 1765 and whose wall monument can be seen at the west end of the north aisle.

## ⓘ information

### Contact details

St James Garlickhythe
Garlick Hill
London, EC4V 2AL

 +44 (0)20 7236 1719

 **St James Garlickhythe site**
www.stjamesgarlickhythe.org.uk

info@stjamesgarlickhythe.org.uk

### Transport links

⊖ Mansion House;
Cannon Street

# LONDON BRIDGE
## CITY OF LONDON, EC4

See map p.53 **(12)**

##  A TRAGEDY FROM LONG AGO

Old London Bridge began construction in 1176 and used to stand a little further down river from the current span. It was far more than just a simple crossing and was lined with houses and stores on both sides of the roadway. The churchyard of St Magnus the Martyr provided pedestrian access to it, and there is a long-held tradition that the reach of the Thames that flows past the church is haunted by ghostly cries.

In 1290, Edward I ordered the expulsion of all Jews from England. One group hired a ship to take them abroad, and it was arranged with the captain that they would set sail from just below London Bridge. However, their vessel was caught on an ebb tide and became beached upon the river sands. The captain suggested that everyone leave the ship to wait for the turn of the tide on a nearby sandbank. As the tide began to rise, the captain and crew raced back to the ship, leaving the hapless passengers to drown in the rising waters. The exact spot where the callous event occurred is uncertain, but there is a strong Jewish tradition that it was beneath London Bridge.

The ghostly screams of the victims are said to echo down the centuries, and, according to one Anglo–Jewish writer, Mr. Margoliouth, the spot where it happened "is under the influence of ceaseless rage; and however calm and serene the river is elsewhere, the place is furiously boisterous."

## (i) information

### Contact details
London Bridge
City of London
London, EC4

### Transport links
⊖ London Bridge

# TOWER OF LONDON
## TOWER HILL, EC3

See map p.53 (13)

## ☞ ENGLAND'S MOST HAUNTED BUILDING

Grim, gray, and awe-inspiring, the Tower has dominated the London landscape since its construction by William the Conqueror in 1078. Today, it is perhaps the most haunted building in England.

The White Tower is the oldest and most forbidding of all the Tower's buildings and its winding stone corridors are the eerie haunt of a "White Lady," who once stood at a window waving to a group of children in the building opposite. It may well be her cheap perfume that impregnates the air around the entrance to St John's Chapel.

The Bloody Tower is home to the most poignant shades that drift through this dreadful fortress. When Edward IV died suddenly in April 1483, his 12-year-old son was destined to succeed him as Edward V. However, before the boy's coronation could take place, both he and his younger brother, Richard, were declared illegitimate by Parliament. Their uncle, the Duke of

▼ *The site of royal executions, the Tower of London is haunted by its victims.*

Gloucester ascended the throne as Richard III. The boys, meanwhile, had been sent to the Tower of London, ostensibly in preparation for Edward's coronation. But, in about June 1483, they mysteriously vanished and were never seen alive again.

Many believed that they had been murdered on Richard's instructions and that their bodies were buried somewhere within the grounds of the Tower.

When two skeletons were uncovered beneath a staircase of the White Tower in 1674, they were presumed to be the remains of the two princes and were afforded royal burial in Westminster Abbey. Since then, the whimpering wraiths of the two children, dressed in white nightgowns and clutching each other in terror, have frequently been seen in the dimly lit rooms of their imprisonment.

(i) information

### Contact details

Tower of London
London, EC3N 4AB

☎ 0844 482 7777 (UK)
+44 (0)20 3166 6000 (non UK)

 Tower of London site
www.hrp.org.uk/TowerOfLondon
VisitorServices_TOL@hrp.org.uk

### Transport links

⊖ Tower Hill

# ALL HALLOWS BY THE TOWER
BYWARD STREET, EC3

See map p.53 (14)

## 👉 THE LADY IN BLACK

A few days before the Christmas of 1920, a choirmaster and two choirboys had been singing in the church of All Hallows by the Tower for about 20 minutes when they noticed an old lady standing a short distance away from them.

She was dressed in old-fashioned clothing, her hair was gray and her face had sallow features. She seemed so real that one of the boys offered her a chair to sit on and the woman nodded her thanks and sat down.

Their strange visitor mystified the choirmaster. He had locked the door when they had entered, so how could she have got inside? Just as their practice concluded, the mysterious visitor vanished suddenly.

Five years later, the choirmaster was approached by an old man one Sunday morning who told him that when he had been a choirboy, some 60 years before, a somewhat eccentric lady organist with a passion for carols had led the choir in those days. The gentleman's description corresponded to the apparition exactly. Could it have been the ghost of the former choirmistress that had appeared in the church on that December night?

◀ *An eccentric lady organist from the mid-19th century has been known to appear at the church.*

## ⓘ information

### Contact details

All Hallows by
the Tower
Byward Street
London, EC3R 5BJ

☎ +44 (0)20 7481 2928

 All Hallows by
the Tower site
www.ahbtt.org.uk

parish@ahbtt.org.uk

### Transport links

 Tower Hill

# BANK UNDERGROUND STATION

PRINCES STREET, EC3

See map p.53

##  THE STENCH FROM BEYOND THE GRAVE

Bank Underground station sits at the historic hub of the City of London and has long been reported by maintenance workers as a focus for supernatural activity. Here, in the early hours of some mornings they complain of being overcome by a foul stench—"like the smell of an open grave."

In the wake of the repugnant smell there comes a dreadful feeling of foreboding and melancholy. This experience may be connected with the fact that the next station along the line, Liverpool Street, is believed to have been built on the site of a 17th-century plague pit.

Could it be possible that something from all the decomposing bodies that were buried together has impregnated the soil around the station?

And, when conditions are right, does some form of miasma steep down into the tunnel and drift toward Bank Station?

---

## (i) information

### Contact details

Bank Underground Station
Princes Street
City of London, EC3V 3LA

 +44 (0)20 7222 1234

[www] **London guide site**
www.londontown.com
/LondonInformation
/Underground_Stations
/Bank/3bc2

### Transport links

⊖ Bank

# BANK OF ENGLAND

## THREADNEEDLE STREET, EC2

See map p.53 **16**

 ## THE BANK NUN

On November 2, 1811, Philip Whitehead, who had been employed in the cashier's office at the Bank of England, was brought to the dock of the Old Bailey and charged with forgery. Found guilty, he was sentenced to death and was duly hanged in early 1812. However, the news of his crime and execution was kept from his devoted sister, Sarah Whitehead. She was removed by Philip's friends to a house in Wine Office Court, off Fleet Street.

One day, Sarah turned up at the bank to enquire about her brother's whereabouts, and an unthinking clerk told her what had happened. The shock of the discovery made her lose her mind and thereafter she turned up at the bank daily to ask after her brother.

She became known as the "Bank Nun" on account of her peculiar attire, which consisted of a long black dress and a crepe veil.

Convinced that the bank's governors were keeping an immense fortune from her, Sarah accused them of defrauding her. By 1818, the bank's governors had grown sufficiently tired of her daily disturbances to so give her a sum of money on the condition that she never return to the bank again.

In life, Sarah honored that contract, but in death her wraith has broken it many times. More than one late-night wanderer, wending his or her weary way home along Threadneedle Street has been surprised by her ghostly figure.

## (i) information

### Contact details

Bank of England
Threadneedle Street
London, EC2R 8AH

 +44 (0)20 7601 4444

www Bank of England site
www.bankofengland.co.uk

enquiries@bankofengland.co.uk

### Transport links

 Bank

# 78 ST BOTOLPH'S CHURCH

## BISHOPSGATE, EC2

See map p.53

## ☞ THE GHOST IN THE PHOTOGRAPH

In 1982, photographer Chris Brackley took a picture inside this historic old City church. The only people present at the time were him and his wife. When the photograph

▼ *The ghostly figure in Chris Brackley's photograph.*

was developed, he was astonished to note that a woman in old-fashioned garb was standing on the balcony to the right of the altar.

The negative was subjected to expert analysis, which revealed that there was no double exposure to the film and it was also proved that Chris's equipment was not faulty.

A few years later, Chris was contacted by a builder, who had previously undertaken restoration work in St Botolph's crypt. He explained to the photographer that he had inadvertently disturbed a pile of old coffins when knocking down a wall. One had come open to reveal a well-preserved body, the face of which bore an uncanny resemblance to the figure in Chris's photograph.

---

## ⓘ information

---

### Contact details

St Botolph's Church
Bishopsgate
London, EC2M 3TL

☎ +44 (0)20 7588 3388

 **St Botolph's site**
www.botolph.org.uk

church@botolph.org.uk

### Transport links

⊖ Liverpool Street

# WESTMINSTER TO KNIGHTSBRIDGE

Westminster is home to a diverse collection of apparitions. From the ghostly soldier in Westminster Abbey to the headless specter that occasionally rises from the tranquil waters of the lake in St James's Park. This chapter includes the ghosts that haunt the residence of Britain's Prime Minister, and looks at the two phantoms that roam the rooms and corridors of Buckingham Palace. Heading west we discuss the haunting at the Royal Albert Hall before moving on to England's most haunted bed!

## HAUNTED LOCATIONS

(1) Cleopatra's Needle

(2) Admiralty Building

(3) The Adelphi Arches

(4) Davenports Magic

(5) 10 Downing Street

(6) St James's Park

(7) 19 St James's Place

(8) Westminster Bridge

(9) Clarence House

(10) Buckingham Palace

(11) Westminster Abbey

(12) Eaton Place

(13) The Grenadier

(14) St James's Palace

(15) Montpelier Square

(16) Royal Albert Hall

(17) Victoria and Albert Museum

# CLEOPATRA'S NEEDLE

VICTORIA EMBANKMENT, WC2

See map p.81 (1)

##  A MYSTERIOUS ENCOUNTER

This mysterious obelisk, which dates to 1450BC, was brought to London from Alexandria in 1878 and has stood proudly on the banks of the river Thames ever since.

Reportedly, more suicides occur on the reach of the Thames that flows past it than on any other part of the river. People passing the column at night have occasionally been startled by the sound of a low moaning, which they hear emanating from within the dark granite.

One of the most mysterious events to have occurred in the vicinity of this most enigmatic of monuments took place on a foggy night in the 1940s, when a hysterical young woman suddenly approached a policeman crossing over Waterloo Bridge.

She told him that someone was about to jump into the Thames and begged him to help her prevent the tragedy. The constable followed her through the dense fog and arrived at Cleopatra's Needle just in time to stop a young woman from throwing herself into the murky waters of the racing river.

As he pulled the suicidal woman back from the brink, he was astonished to find himself face to face with the same young woman who had led him to this place. Turning back to where she had been standing, he could find no trace of her.

 *More suicides take place close to Cleopatra's Needle than on any other stretch of the river Thames. Could it have anything to do with the low moan that passers-by have reported in the late evening?*

## (i) information

### Contact details

Cleopatra's Needle
Victoria Embankment,
close to Embankment
Underground station

 **Historic UK site**

www.historic-uk.com
/HistoryUK/England-History
/CleopatrasNeedle.htm

### Transport links

⊖ Embankment;
Charing Cross

**84**

# ADMIRALTY BUILDING
WHITEHALL, SW1                    See map p.81

## ☞ MARTHA RAY THE POLITICIAN'S FRIEND

The dark brick Admiralty Building was built in the 1720s by architect Thomas Ripley and was later extended to become Admiralty House, home of the First Lord of the Admiralty.

In the latter half of the 18th century, the office was held by John Montagu, 4th Earl of Sandwich, who brought his mistress, Martha Ray, to live there with him.

Having borne the Earl several children, Martha embarked on an affair with James Hackman, a penniless army lieutenant. Although the two fell deeply in love, Hackman lacked the means to support Martha. When she refused to leave the Earl, her heartbroken lover left the army and became an equally impecunious clergyman.

One night in April 1779, Hackman spotted Miss Ray passing along Whitehall en route to a performance of *Love in a Village* at the Covent Garden Theatre. Insane with jealousy, he rushed home to get a pair of pistols with which, he later claimed, he intended to shoot himself before the eyes of his former mistress. Instead, he shot Martha dead as she emerged from the theater. The crime was witnessed by virtually the entire audience of the play. The passion of the crime together with the romance of the story, thrilled polite society. The Earl of Sandwich, in a gesture of moving forgiveness, provided Hackman with financial assistance during his imprisonment and trial. Found guilty, Hackman was sentenced to death and subsequently executed.

Martha Ray has haunted Admiralty House ever since her murder and was seen in the early 20th century by former British prime ministers Winston Churchill and Harold Macmillan.

In June 1969, several newspapers reported that Denis Healey—then Secretary for Defense, who was occupying quarters in the building at the time—was being visited by her restless wraith. Healey was reported to have seen her ghost on several occasions and even went as far as to tell reporters that his children, far from being frightened by her, were actually very fond of "the lady" and had come to accept her as part of the family!

 *Murdered actress Martha Ray has made many a ghostly return to the Admiralty Building on Whitehall. Even Winston Churchill reported seeing her.*

---

## (i) information

---

### Contact details

Admiralty Building
26 Whitehall
Westminster
London, SW1A 2WH

 **London guide site**

www.londonopenhouse.org
/public/london/find
/detail.asp?loh_id=14993

### Transport links

Embankment;
Charing Cross; Piccadilly;
Westminster

**86**

# THE ADELPHI ARCHES
## LOWER ROBERT STREET, WC2

See map p.81

###  POOR JENNY'S ETERNAL DEATH THROES

The delightfully gloomy Lower Robert Street descends into one of the only surviving 18th-century arches in London.

This was built to support the buildings of The Adelphi—a prestigious housing development constructed in 1768 by the Adams brothers. By the 19th century, according to one account, "the most abandoned characters … often passed the night [here], nestling upon foul straw; and many a street thief escaped from his pursuers in these dismal haunts …"

In *David Copperfield*, author Charles Dickens has the protagonist recall: "I was fond of wandering about the Adelphi, because it was a mysterious place with those dark arches …"

The ambience of this subterranean vault is still sufficient to elicit cold shivers from visitors, and it comes as little surprise to find that this place of silent shadow is haunted.

One of the desperate characters to whom the arches became home was "Poor Jenny," a Victorian prostitute who was strangled by one of her clients on the grim bundle of filthy rags that she used as her bed. Today, Jenny's terrifying, pain-racked screams can be heard, followed by a rhythmic drumming, as her feet repeat her death tattoo upon the flagstones. The sound shatters the stillness and chills the marrow of those who happen to be in the vicinity.

---

## ⓘ information

### Contact details

The Adelphi Arches
Lower Robert Street
Westminster
London, WC2

### Transport links

⊖ Charing Cross

# DAVENPORTS MAGIC

## CHARING CROSS UNDERGROUND ARCADE, WC2   See map p.81 (4)

##  THE VANISHING SPECTER

Davenports is the oldest family magic business in the world, and from the moment the dull thud of a loud bell announces one's arrival, one gets the sensation of having entered a truly hidden gem of secret London. A veritable cornucopia of all things magical and mysterious confronts you. Ferocious-looking arm choppers, complete with plastic severed limbs, among other things, glimmer behind glass display cases.

The store is haunted by what the staff maintain is a "male presence." Several of the assistants, who demonstrate their dexterous skills at sleight of hand before wide-eyed visitors, have caught glimpses of someone walking to the side of the counter toward the stock room. However, whenever they go to investigate, there is never anyone there.

At other times, items have been moved around in the storeroom, which can prove a little annoying for staff trying to despatch an urgent order. This latter activity though is easily dealt with by simply asking the ghost to return whatever object it is that has disappeared.

---

## (i) information

### Contact details

Davenports Magic
7 Charing Cross
  Underground Arcade
Strand
London, WC2N 4HZ

 +44 (0)300 061 2000

**Davenports Magic site**

www.davenportsmagic.co.uk

all@davenportsmagic.co.uk

### Transport links

Charing Cross;
Embankment

# 10 DOWNING STREET

DOWNING STREET, SW1

See map p.81 (5)

##  THE PRIME MINISTER'S HAUNTED ABODE

Several ghosts are known to haunt 10 Downing Street—the home and office to successive British prime ministers. One is a man in Regency-style clothing who makes fleeting appearances both inside and outside the house. Nobody knows who he is, although there is a suggestion that he may be a former prime minister.

During extensive alterations made to the building in the late 1950s, workmen are said to have encountered the ghost several times. On one occasion his shimmering shade was even seen in the garden, where it moved toward the wall that backs onto Horse Guards Parade before promptly disappearing.

A lady in a long dress and wearing a magnificent set of pearls haunts the Pillared Drawing Room, which is used today for official functions and the signing of international agreements. Several messengers as well as people working in the neighboring offices have reported both seeing and hearing her phantom.

The basement of 10 Downing Street is the spectral realm of a little girl who has been known to hold the hands of those walking along its corridors. It is also where several employees have reported smelling the overpoweringly strong odor of cigar smoke wafting around the rooms. This has led some to wonder if the ghost of former prime minister Winston Churchill might be in residence and enjoying the odd cigar from time to time.

 *The smell of tobacco wafting through the basement of 10 Downing Street has been attributed to the ghost of a cigar-smoking Winston Churchill.*

---

## (i) information

---

**Contact details**

10 Downing Street
London, SW1 2AA

[www] **10 Downing Street site**
www.number10.gov.uk

**Transport links**

⊖ Westminster;
Embankment

# 90 ST JAMES'S PARK

### HORSE GUARDS ROAD, SW1

See map p.81 ⑥

## ☞ THE HEADLESS LADY OF THE LAKE

St James's Park was originally laid out for James I in 1603. The lake was remodeled between 1826 and 1827 by the Regency architect John Nash, by which time it had already acquired the spectral resident that has chilled the blood of many a late night

wanderer. A headless woman has been seen rising from the rippling waters of the lake. She drifts slowly onto dry land, where she suddenly breaks into a frenzied run, her arms flailing wildly about her. Petrified onlookers stand, rooted to the spot, as the apparition rushes into the bushes and disappears.

In life, the phantom figure is thought to have been the wife of a sergeant of the Coldstream Guards, murdered and decapitated by her husband, with her head buried at a secret location and her body flung into "The Canal," as the lake was then called. Since that day, her headless cadaver has roamed St James's Park, a restless phantom condemned to search in vain for her missing head.

## ⓘ information

### Contact details

St. James's Park
London, SW1A 2BJ

 +44 (0)20 7298 2000

 **Royal Parks site**
www.royalparks.org.uk
/parks/st_james_park/

hq@royalparks.gsi.gov.uk

### Transport links

 St. James's Park

# 19 ST JAMES'S PLACE

ST JAMES'S PLACE, SW1                    See map p.81 (7)

##  WHEN DEATH'S HERALD CAME

For much of the 19th century, 19 St James's Place was owned by two spinster sisters, Ann and Harriet Pearson. The two women were deeply devoted to one another, and when Ann died in 1858 Harriet opted to live alone in the house they had shared together for so long.

In November 1864, Harriet was taken seriously ill while visiting relations in Brighton, Sussex. She was brought back to her house in London, and her two nieces, Mrs. Coppinger and Miss Emma Pearson, and her nephew's wife Mrs. John Pearson moved in to nurse her.

On December 23 of that year, a heavy snowstorm swept across the capital and a thick mist descended upon St James's Place. Mrs. Coppinger and Miss Emma retired to bed, leaving Mrs. John Pearson to look after their ailing aunt. At around 1 am both of the women were suddenly woken by a movement in the room. They were shocked to see their deceased aunt drift past their door, apparently heading for the sick room. Then, Mrs. John Pearson came rushing into their room in a state of great agitation, having also seen and recognized the ghost of Ann Pearson. She reported that she had seen the apparition enter the room and cross to Harriet's bedside.

Nervously the three women returned to Harriet's room, where they found her awake. She told them that her sister Ann's ghost had just come to her in order to call her away. Shortly afterward, the old lady slipped into a coma and, having lingered for most of that day, Harriet died in the early evening.

---

## (i) information

### Contact details

19 St James's Place
London, SW1A

### Transport links

 Green Park

# WESTMINSTER BRIDGE
## WESTMINSTER, SW1

See map p.81 **8**

##  THE GHOSTLY LEAP OF JACK THE RIPPER

If you stand on Westminster Bridge on December 31 and look eastward as midnight approaches, you may well be rewarded with a sighting of the ghost of one of London's most enigmatic criminals.

There is a local tradition that, as the first chimes of the clock Big Ben usher in the New Year, a shadowy figure will suddenly materialize on the parapet and leap headlong into the murky waters of the river Thames below.

Legend maintains that this is the hour when Jack the Ripper killed himself by plunging into the river from this spot in 1888, and that every year since, his wraith has been condemned to repeat his descent into infamy over and over again.

Should a new year visit be out of the question a spectral barge has been known to drift toward the bridge on misty fall mornings. The boat passes beneath the bridge and vanishes before reaching the other side.

*Stand on Westminster Bridge at midnight on New Year's Eve and you may be lucky enough to see the ghost of the serial killer Jack the Ripper.*

---

## ⓘ information

### Contact details
Westminster Bridge
Westminster
London, SW1

### Transport links
⊖ Westminster

94

# CLARENCE HOUSE
## THE MALL, SW1

See map p.81  **9**

##  THE OLD DUKE OF CONNAUGHT

Built in 1825 for the Duke of Clarence, who later became William IV, Clarence House was for many years the London home of Her Majesty Queen Elizabeth The Queen Mother. Following her death in 2002, the house became the abode of her beloved grandson Prince Charles.

The ghost that is reputed to haunt Clarence House is that of Arthur, Duke of Connaught, the third son of Queen Victoria. He lived here from 1900 until his death in 1942.

During World War II, the house was transformed into the offices for the Foreign Relations Department of the British Red Cross Society. One Saturday afternoon, a year or so after the duke's death, a recently employed clerk named Sonia Marsh was working alone in the vast building. She became decidedly uneasy and was convinced that someone—or something—was watching her. Peering into the darkness beyond her desk, she saw a grayish, misty, triangular shape drifting toward her. Petrified, Sonia leapt to her feet, grabbed her coat and rushed from the building as fast as she could. When Sonia returned to work on the following Monday morning, she told a colleague of her experience.

"Oh don't worry," came the reassuring reply, "It was probably the old Duke of Connaught. We see him all the time!"

## (i) information

### Contact details

Clarence House
The Mall
London, SW1 1BA

 +44 (0)20 7766 7303

 **Royal Collection site**
www.royalcollection.org.uk

### Transport links

Green Park;
St James's Park;
Trafalgar Square

# BUCKINGHAM PALACE

**95**

BUCKINGHAM PALACE ROAD, SW1

See map p.81

##  THE FESTIVE SPECTER

Built in 1703 for John Sheffield, the Duke of Buckingham, Buckingham House became a royal palace when it came into the ownership of George III. Queen Victoria, however, was the first monarch to actually live in the palace and since then it has been the principal London home of all her successors.

Tradition maintains that, long before the palace was built, a monk at the monastery that once occupied the site was involved in an indiscretion that resulted in his being starved to death in the punishment cell. Presumably his death occurred over the festive period as his ghost only returns to haunt the palace on Christmas Day.

The monk always appears on the terrace that overlooks the gardens to the rear of the building. Bound in heavy chains, he clanks and moans his way along the terrace for a few chilling moments, before fading away.

---

## (i) information

### Contact details

Buckingham Palace
Buckingham Palace Road
London, SW1A 1AA

☎ +44 (0)20 7766 7300

 Royal Collection site
www.royalcollection.org.uk

### Transport links

⊖ St James's Park; Victoria

🚆 Victoria

# WESTMINSTER ABBEY

DEAN'S YARD, SW1

See map p.81 (11)

##  A GHOSTLY MONK & THE UNKNOWN WARRIOR

Over the centuries, Westminster Abbey has been considerably expanded and altered and, in the process, the level of the floor has been progressively lowered. This may explain why the ghostly monk who is known to haunt the building is seen floating a little way off the ground. He is known as "Father Benedictus" and is most often viewed bobbing around the cloisters in the early evening. His spectral figure appears quite solid, and he has been known to hold conversations with witnesses, many of whom do not realize that he is anything other than flesh and blood.

In 1900, the monk kept a group of visitors entertained for a good 25 minutes as he drifted around the cloisters before backing slowly toward a wall, where he melted into the fabric. In 1932, two American visitors even held a long conversation with him, later commenting that they found him to be extremely polite.

Westminster Abbey's Tomb of the Unknown Warrior—a poignant memorial to the soldiers who died in World War I—is another spot within the Abbey that has been known for its ghostly activity.

From time to time when the crowds have left, a spectral soldier materializes alongside the tomb and stands for a few minutes with his head bowed, before slowly dissolving into thin air.

◀ *The ghosts of a monk and soldier can sometimes be seen at Westminster Abbey.*

## (i) information

### Contact details

Westminster Abbey
20 Dean's Yard
London, SW1P 3PA

☎ +44 (0)20 7222 5152

 **Westminster Abbey site**
www.westminster-abbey.org

### Transport links

⊖ Westminster;
St James's Park;
Embankment

 Charing Cross

## 98 EATON PLACE
BELGRAVIA, SW1

See map p.81  **12**

### ☞ THE ADMIRAL'S DOPPELGÄNGER

On June 22, 1893, Admiral, Sir George Tryon was on maneuvers with the Mediterranean Fleet off the coast of Syria. When he gave orders for his ship the *Victoria* and the nearby *Camperdown* to turn inward and steam toward each other it was obvious to all on board that disaster was imminent. However, none of his subordinates dared question Tryon's extraordinary command. In consequence, the two ships collided and the *Victoria* sank, taking the Admiral and 400 mariners to a watery grave. As the ship went down, Sir George was heard to say: "It is entirely my fault."

At more or less the exact moment that Sir George Tryon was plummeting to the ocean bed, his wife was holding an "at home" in their house in Eaton Place in London. Suddenly Sir George, resplendent in his full naval regalia, appeared before the more than 100 guests, strolled across the room and vanished.

Lady Tryon did not see him herself. She was mystified when she was told by her guests of her husband's appearance. She explained that he was far away at sea. Next day, however, word reached Lady Tryon of the tragedy and she realized that her guests must have seen her husband's ghost.

---

## ⓘ information

### Contact details
Eaton Place
Belgravia
London, SW1X

### Transport links
 Sloane Square; Victoria

 Victoria

# THE GRENADIER
## WILTON ROW, SW1

See map p.81 (13)

##  THE OFFICER RETURNS

Wilton Mews is a delightful hidden nook that is tucked away from the rush of modern London and has a decidedly country-village air about it. Colorful cottages line the cobblestones and nestling within its tranquil serenity is one of London's most enchanting pubs, The Grenadier. Reputedly, the pub's upper floors were once used as the officers' mess of a nearby barracks, while its cellar was pressed into service as a drinking and gambling lair for the common soldiers.

It is here that a young subaltern is said to have been caught cheating at cards. His comrades punished him with such a savage beating that he died from his injuries.

Although the year in which this occurred is not known, the month it happened is believed to have been September, as this is when the pub experiences an onslaught of supernatural activity.

A solemn, silent specter has been seen moving slowly across the low-ceilinged rooms. Objects either disappear or else are mysteriously moved overnight. Unseen hands rattle tables and chairs, and a strange, icy chill has been known to hang in the air, sometimes for days on end. Footsteps have been heard pacing anxiously around empty rooms, while every so often a low, sighing moan has been heard emanating from the depths of the cellar.

---

## (i) information

### Contact details

The Grenadier
18 Wilton Row
Knightsbridge
London, SW1X 7NR

 +44 (0)20 7235 3074

 London guide site
www.viewlondon.co.uk
/pubsandbars/grenadier-
info-6463.html

### Transport links

⊖ Hyde Park Corner

**100**

# ST JAMES'S PALACE
## ST JAMES'S STREET, SW1

See map p.81 **(14)**

##  THE SMELL OF GHOSTLY BLOOD

St James's Palace's most famous haunting dates from the first half of the 19th century. In the early hours of May 31, 1810, Ernest Augustus, Duke of Cumberland, was subjected to a ferocious attack, as a sharp blade began slashing him. He screamed for help and his valet Cornelius Neale rushed to assist him. He found the duke's regimental saber lying on the floor by the door, covered in blood.

A doctor was summoned, and, as his wounds were being treated, Cumberland asked for his other valet, Joseph Sellis, to be sent for. Two servants went to rouse him, but found him lying dead on his bed with his throat slashed. A hastily convened inquest concluded that the dead valet had, for reasons unknown, attempted to murder his master, and had returned to his room to commit suicide in remorse.

However, some courtiers believed that Cumberland had actually murdered Sellis and pointed out that the valet's hands were found to be clean although there was bloodstained water in his washbasin. One theory was that Sellis had found the duke in bed with his wife and, in an ensuing struggle, had been murdered to stop him exposing Cumberland's adultery.

Whatever the truth, there are occasions when the ghost of Sellis has been seen walking the palace corridors, a gaping wound across his throat, the sickly sweet smell of fresh blood trailing in his wake.

*St .James's Palace is haunted by the shade of Joseph Sellis with his throat slashed.* ▶

---

##  information

### Contact details

St James's Palace
St James's Street
London, SW1

 **St James's Palace site**
www.royal.gov.uk
/TheRoyalResidences
/StJamessPalace
/StJamessPalace.aspx

### Transport links

 Green Park;
St James's Park

# MONTPELIER SQUARE

KNIGHTSBRIDGE, SW7                      See map p.81  15

##  SHE CAME BACK TO SAVE HER HUSBAND'S SOUL

In 1913, a vicar was leaving church when a lady approached him to tell him that a man living nearby was seriously ill and that he wished to consult with a man of God. The clergyman went with her to a waiting taxicab and the two were driven to an imposing house in Montpelier Square.

The butler who answered the door said that his master was in good health and certainly had no need of the priest's services. Mystified, the vicar looked round for an explanation, but there was no sign of the woman. At that moment the owner of the house appeared at the door and invited the vicar inside. "It is very strange," said the man, "that you have been sent on such an errand in such a mysterious way … though I am perfectly well, I have been troubled lately about the state of my soul, and I have been seriously contemplating calling upon you …"

The clergyman stayed for a few hours as the man unburdened his conscience, and it was agreed that he would come to church the next morning.

However, the man failed to appear at church, and so the vicar returned to the house to see what the matter was. He discovered that the man had dropped dead just 10 minutes after he had left him the previous evening. The vicar was led up to the room where the man's body lay and happened to notice a portrait of the lady who had fetched him to the house the previous evening. "Who is this?" he asked. "That sir," replied the butler, "is my master's wife, who died 15 years ago."

---

##  information

**Contact details**

Montpelier Square
Knightsbridge
London, SW7

 **London guide site**

www.londontown.com
/LondonStreets
/montpelier_square_94a.html

**Transport links**

Knightsbridge

# ROYAL ALBERT HALL

KENSINGTON GORE, SW7

See map p.81

##  FATHER WILLIS & THE LADIES OF THE NIGHT

The Royal Albert Hall stands on the site of Gore House, the former home of Marguerite, Countess of Blessingdon.

The Royal Commissioners for the Great Exhibition purchased the property, demolished the house and built the Royal Albert Hall on the site in commemoration of Queen Victoria's husband Prince Albert. The venue has been in continuous use since it was opened in March 1871.

Several ghosts are said to haunt the building. The first is that of Henry "Father" Willis, who designed the 150-ton (152-tonne) organ, which had an impressive 9,000 pipes and was the largest instrument of its kind when it was built. Dressed in Victorian clothing, his ghost has been seen wandering around the hall at night.

The building's other specters support the belief that Gore House was at one time used as a brothel prior to its demolition. Each November, two Victorian "ladies of the night" are said to roam along the upper gallery level of the hall and can be seen walking into one of the ladies' bathrooms. They walk along arm in arm and remain happily oblivious to any who encounter them.

##  information

### Contact details

Royal Albert Hall
Kensington Gore
London, SW7 2AP

 0845 401 5045 (UK)
+44 (0)20 7589 8212 (non UK)

Royal Albert Hall site
www.royalalberthall.com

### Transport links

South Kensington;
High Street Kensington

104

# VICTORIA AND ALBERT MUSEUM
CROMWELL ROAD, SW7

See map p.81

##  THE GREAT BED OF WARE

On display in the Victoria and Albert Museum, this impressive piece of furniture has the dubious distinction of being the most haunted bed in Britain.

Although it actually dates from about 1590, legend has it that the bed was made especially for King Edward IV by carpenter Jonas Fosbrooke in 1463 and intended for the sole use of the monarch.

When Edward's son, Edward V, became one of the tragic "Princes in the Tower," the bed was sold and passed through the bedrooms of a succession of inns at Ware in Hertfordshire.

On one occasion in the 17th century, 12 married couples are reputed to have shared the bed during a festival when there was literally, no room at the inn!

However, the delightfully stuffy spirit of Fosbrooke did not take kindly to riff-raff enjoying the luxury of his creation. He disturbed the slumber of anyone who dared to sleep in the bed by pinching and scratching them in a most unpleasant manner. Indeed, so well known were his attacks that it was once customary for guests at the various inns to drink a toast to the bed and the ghost before retiring for the night.

*Those who sleep on the Bed of Ware may be troubled during the night by the spirit of its creator.*

---

## ⓘ information

**Contact details**

Victoria and Albert Museum
Cromwell Road
London, SW7 2RL

 +44 (0)20 7942 2000

 **Victoria and Albert Museum site**

www.vam.ac.uk

**Transport links**

⊖ South Kensington;
Knightsbridge

THE GREAT BED OF WARE

# WEST LONDON

In this chapter, we delve into the ghosts that haunt London's western suburbs. Kensington Palace and Holland House give up their spectral secrets before we head to Notting Hill and an encounter with what must surely be one of England's most bizarre hauntings: a phantom double-decker bus. We also head out to the glorious Chiswick House, where the chance of a ghostly breakfast is not to be sniffed at.

## HAUNTED LOCATIONS

1. Kensington Palace
2. Holland House
3. Coronet Cinema
4. Cambridge Gardens
5. Walpole House
6. St Paul's Churchyard
7. St Dunstan's church
8. St Nicholas Church
9. Chiswick House

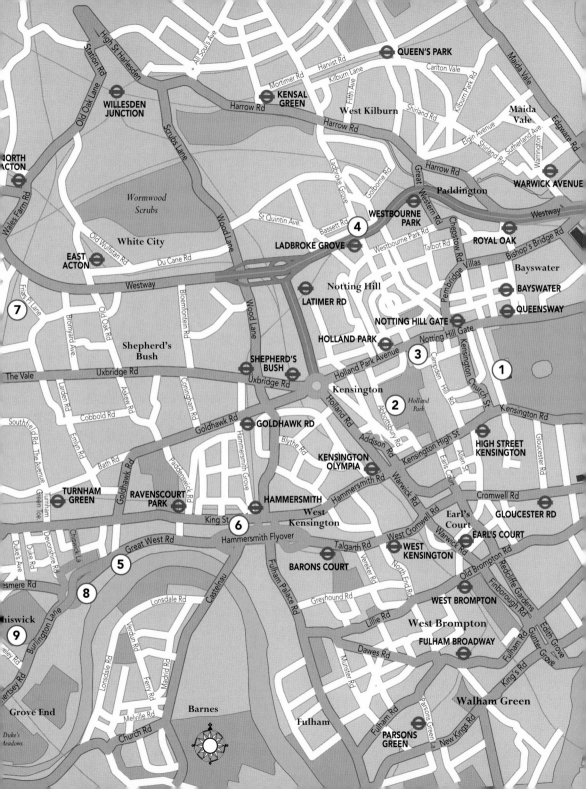

# KENSINGTON PALACE

KENSINGTON GARDENS, W8 See map p.107 **1**

## ☞ WHY DON'T THEY COME?

Beginning life as a Jacobean mansion, this house became a royal palace in 1689, when William III bought it in the hope that its pastoral location would alleviate his chronic asthma. Architects Sir Christopher Wren and Nicholas Hawksmoor subsequently renovated the building and, following William's death in 1702, Queen Anne took up residence at the palace.

In the 18th century, George I and George II both chose Kensington Palace as their favored London home.

George II's last days were spent at Kensington Palace, anxiously awaiting long overdue despatches from Hanover. Hour after hour, he would cast a hopeful glance up at the weathervane that stood over the entrance, hoping to see the wind change direction and speed his messengers to him. His courtiers would often hear his agitated voice sounding from his chamber, as he called out in his broken, heavily accented English: "Why don't they come?" His wishes remained unfulfilled for, by the time the wind did change direction, the king had passed away.

George II's ghost still returns to the palace, where his fretful face often appears at the window of his chamber, gazing up toward the weathervane. And every so often his voice is heard echoing along the corridors crying: "Why don't they come?"

During the reign of George III, several members of the royal family lived at Kensington Palace. Among them was the king's fifth daughter, Princess Sophia.

Sophia fell deeply in love with Thomas Garth, a royal equerry, and bore him an illegitimate son. However, Garth's ardor waned soon after the birth and poor Sophia retreated into a reclusive existence in her apartments at Kensington Palace.

As the years passed, her eyesight began to fail, and her only solace in her old age was to sit at her spinning wheel or toil at her embroidery frame. Although she died at nearby York House, her spirit returns to Kensington Palace, where the sound of a ghostly spinning wheel, cranked by an invisible hand, has been heard creaking in the early hours of some mornings.

 *The ghost of George II still calls for news of despatches from Hanover at Kensington Palace.*

## (i) information

### Contact details

Kensington Palace
Kensington Gardens
London, W8 4PX

 0844 482 7777 (UK)

**Historic Royal Palaces site**

www.hrp.org.uk
/KensingtonPalace

### Transport links

⊖ High Street Kensington;
Queensway

# 110 HOLLAND HOUSE
HOLLAND WALK, W8 See map p.107 ②

## ☞ THREE DROPS OF GHOSTLY BLOOD

Holland House was built in 1606 for Sir Walter Cope, Chancellor of the Exchequer to James I. Although it was devastated by bombing in World War II, enough of its façade has survived to remind us of what a fairy-tale place it must have been.

In his will, Cope left the house to his wife, on the condition that she did not remarry. When she did, the house passed to their daughter Lady Rich, whose husband, Henry, was created Earl of Holland in 1624. The Earl was beheaded for his royalist sympathies during the English Civil War and the house was confiscated, but it was later restored to Lady Holland and passed down through successive generations

▼ *The ghost of the 1st Earl of Holland can sometimes be seen wandering around the building after midnight.*

of the family until Henry Fox, 1st Baron Holland, purchased it in 1763.

It was during the tenure of the 3rd Baron Holland that the glory days of Holland House commenced. His wife, Elizabeth Vassall, entertained an impressive selection of the great, good, and infamous at their house, including William IV, Lord Byron, Benjamin Disraeli, and Lord Macaulay, to name but a few. Charles Dickens, who became a close friend, was once moved to wonder who would take the place of these rare personalities when they had "stepped into the shadow."

Today, the King George Memorial Youth Hostel occupies what remains of the building, but the ghost of the 1st Earl of Holland has been known to walk its corridors.

In the past, the Earl's appearances have been presaged by three drops of blood, which appeared alongside a hidden door. Then, as the clock chimed midnight, his

▲ *Henry Rich, 1st Earl of Holland.*

phantom materialized from within the hidden recess, his head tucked under his arm. Drifting about the building, he surveyed the rooms of his old home, until as the first rays of dawn stretched across the grounds, the earl returned to the hidden door to fade away once more.

## ⓘ information

### Contact details

Holland House
Holland Walk
Kensington
London, W8 7QU

### Transport links

⊖ Holland Park;
Notting Hill Gate

**112**

# CORONET CINEMA
NOTTING HILL GATE, W11 See map p.107

## ☞ THE CASHIER WHO FELL FROM GRACE

Boasting one of London's most glorious movie-theater interiors, the Coronet is a true survivor whose majestic Art Nouveau interior is strangely at odds with the Hollywood blockbusters that flicker across its screen today.

In the early 1900s, the building was a successful and popular theater, and it was around this time that it acquired its ghostly resident.

Tradition holds that one of the cashiers was caught taking money from the till and that when she was called into the manager's office to be confronted she let out a scream of despair and raced from the room. She then ran for all she was worth up the stairs to the upper circle, where she flung herself from the balcony and plunged to her death in the well of the theater below.

Since then, the woman's wraith has remained to chill the blood of those who worked at the theater. Indeed, when staff meetings were held in the upper levels of the building, her ghost caused so much disruption that the management was obliged to transfer these meetings to the lower levels.

Agitated footsteps have also been heard racing up the stairs toward the balcony from which she took her plunge. Since the tragic event occurred at Christmas, it is during the festive period that the ghostly activity most often occurs.

---

## ⓘ information

### Contact details

Coronet Cinema
103 Notting Hill Gate
London, W11 3LB

 +44 (0)20 7727 6705

 **Coronet Cinema site**
www.coronet.org

### Transport links

 Notting Hill Gate

# CAMBRIDGE GARDENS
## KENSINGTON, W10

See map p.107 (4)

##  THE PHANTOM BUS

There can be few hauntings that are as bizarre and dramatic as that which afflicts Cambridge Gardens in the early hours of some mornings. The phantom in question is that of a number seven double-decker London bus, which was last seen in May 1990. However, it first came to public attention early one morning in 1934, when a motorist driving along Cambridge Gardens suddenly swerved for no apparent reason and was killed as his car hit a wall and burst into flames.

At the subsequent inquest into the driver's death, witnesses came forward to testify to the existence of a phantom bus, which many of them had seen in more or less the exact spot where the fatal crash had occurred. They told how it would always appear at about 1:15 am (the time that the crash had occurred) and they spoke of their terror as it came racing along the center of the road toward them. No driver was ever visible in the bus, and no lights were ever on. Convinced that they were about to experience a head-on collision with the vehicle, motorists would swerve out of its path and the bus would thunder past them. However, whenever they turned around to look at the bus, they always found that it had vanished without trace.

##  information

### Contact details

Cambridge Gardens
Kensington
London, W10

### Transport links

 Ladbroke Grove

# WALPOLE HOUSE

## CHISWICK MALL, W4

See map p.107 ⑤

### ☞ SHE LONGS ETERNALLY

A past resident of this attractive 16th-century building was the author William Makepeace Thackeray, who immortalized the house as Miss Pinkerton's Academy in his novel *Vanity Fair*. However, it is the ghost of an earlier resident, Barbara Villiers, Duchess of Cleveland, which is said to haunt the building.

Barbara Villiers was one of the greatest beauties of the 17th century and, as such, attracted the roving eye of Charles II, becoming his mistress and bearing him three sons and two daughters.

However, by the time the duchess came to live at Walpole House in 1705, her royal lover was long dead and her appearance had begun to change beyond recognition. She had swollen "gradually to a monstrous bulk," which her physicians diagnosed as dropsy and the two years she spent here proved to be the most miserable of her life. She died on October 9, 1709 at the age of 67.

Her lament at the loss of her beauty appears to have lingered on. Many people walking along Chiswick Mall on nights when the Moon is full, have spied the puffy, bloated face of Barbara Villiers pressed against the glass of Walpole House, her dark eyes rolling in despair, as her restless wraith pursues its eternal quest for the restoration of her long-lost looks.

*Barbara Villiers still stands by the windows of Chiswick's Walpole House imploring her maker to restore her beauty.* ▶

## ⓘ information

### Contact details

Walpole House
Chiswick Mall
Hounslow
London, W4 2PS

 **Mysterious Britain site**
www.mysteriousbritain.co.uk
/england/greater-london
/hauntings/walpole-house-chiswick-mall.html

### Transport links

 Stamford Brook

# ST PAUL'S CHURCHYARD

## QUEEN CAROLINE STREET, W6

See map p.107 (6)

**116**

## ☞ THE GHOST OF REGULAR HABITS

This late 19th-century, Gothic-style church cowers somewhat uneasily alongside the Hammersmith Flyover. Although its churchyard was long ago grassed over, a few old tombs, along with a handful of gravestones, still survive, and it is around these weathered memorials that the Hammersmith ghost is said to appear every 50 years.

A report in the *West London Observer* in July 1955 informed readers that the specter was due to make an appearance the following Wednesday night. This announcement caused something of a local sensation and 400 people turned up in the hope of encountering the apparition. When midnight came and went without so much

as a drop in temperature, the crowd grew bored and quickly dispersed. Fortunately, the *Observer* reporter and a few hardy souls opted to maintain their vigil, and at about 1 am their endeavor was rewarded. A legless figure clad in brilliant white, glided from the church porch and drifted silently toward the tomb where various members of the Fenn and Colvill families lay buried.

The spectators watched, open mouthed, as the figure floated onto the tomb and promptly melted into it. Other witnesses, who had seen the entire episode from a window overlooking the churchyard, observed how a strange wind had rustled the branches of the trees shortly before the ghost had appeared.

---

## ⓘ information

### Contact details

St Paul's Churchyard
Queen Caroline Street
London, W6 9PJ

☎ +44 (0)20 8748 3855

 **St Paul's site**

www.sph.org

info@sph.org

### Transport links

⊖ Hammersmith

# ST DUNSTAN'S CHURCH

FRIAR'S PLACE LANE, W3

See map p.107

##  THE COLOR-CHANGING MONKS

During the middle ages, a monastery stood on the site that is currently occupied by St Dunstan's Church. This may account for the ghostly monks that have been known to manifest themselves before astonished witnesses in several locations about the building.

The Reverend Anton-Stevens, who began his tenure at the church in 1944, and who died in 1966, regularly saw a procession of phantom friars. They appeared wearing brown habits, their hoods pulled up over their heads, drifting along the central aisle toward the altar. He even claimed to have spoken at length with one of the monks, who obligingly dictated an article, which Anton-Stevens subsequently published in the parish magazine.

Kenneth Mason, a reporter with *The Daily Graphic* newspaper, was determined to discover whether the church was haunted or not and so decided to spend one November evening inside the building.

He found the vigil so boring that he fell fast asleep. However, he awoke with a start to find six monks—this time in gray habits—walking toward him. Anxious for a scoop, the fearless reporter rose from his pew and stood right in their path. Unperturbed, the ghostly procession simply walked right through him!

##  information

### Contact details

St Dunstan's Church
Friars Place Lane
Acton
London, W3 7AW

 **St Dunstan's Church site**

www.stdunstanschurch.org.uk

office@stdunstanschurch.org.uk

 +44 (0)20 8743 4117

### Transport links

 Acton Central

Acton

# ST NICHOLAS CHURCH
## CHURCH STREET, W4

See map p.107

## ☞ THE LADIES OF ILLUSTRIOUS BIRTH

Founded in the 15th century, this church's dedication to St Nicholas, the patron saint of sailors and fishermen, remembers the days when Chiswick was a busy riverside fishing village. Although the main body of the church was rebuilt in 1882, the tower remains much as it was 500 years ago.

Among those buried in its churchyard are painter and engraver William Hogarth, artist J. M. Whistler and Barbara Villiers, Duchess of Cleveland (see page 114). Meanwhile, Mary Fauconberg and Frances Rich, the daughters of Oliver Cromwell, lie buried in a vault beneath the church's chancel, along with—so rumor has it—the remains of their father.

It has long been suspected that following Oliver Cromwell's posthumous beheading (see page 37), Mary Fauconberg brought his body to Chiswick, having bribed a guard to let her smuggle her father's headless cadaver away from Tyburn. Here, Cromwell was secretly interred in the vault in which Mary and her sister would eventually be buried.

During the rebuilding of the church in 1882, the Cromwell vault was opened in order to see if there was any veracity in the rumors surrounding Oliver Cromwell's final resting place. Captain Dale, the then-vicar's son, claimed that, along with the coffins of the two sisters, he spied a third coffin, showing signs of rough usage, which was pushed against the far side of the vault.

Cromwell's name still aroused violent emotion at the time, so the vicar took the precaution of having the vault bricked up and left unmarked. He feared that groups of sightseers and protestors might arrive in their droves.

Perhaps it is the fact that their resting place was desecrated by a clergyman, who by his own admission resented everything their father stood for, which has caused the ghosts of the two ladies to roam the churchyard in the hours before dawn. Their white-clad figures drift silently among the graves, until, with the coming of the first light of day, they melt slowly into the fabric of the church and return to their unmarked grave.

▲ *The daughters of Oliver Cromwell, swathed in white, wander the graves of St Nicholas churchyard.*

# ⓘ information

## Contact details

St Nicholas Church
Church Street, Chiswick
London, W4 2PH

☎ +44 (0)20 8995 7876

 **St Nicholas Church site**

www.stnicholaschiswick.org

office@stnicholaschiswick.org

## Transport links

 Turnham Green

 Chiswick

# CHISWICK HOUSE
## BURLINGTON LANE, W4

See map p.107 ⑨

## 👉 THE PHANTOM BREAKFAST

Modeled on the Italian architect Palladio's Villa Rotonda in Vicenza, Italy, Chiswick House was designed by Richard Boyle, 3rd Earl of Burlington, and built between 1725 and 1729. The remarkable building stands as a monument to his appreciation of the arts.

Richard Boyle lived in an adjoining Jacobean mansion, which was demolished in 1758, and used the new house to exhibit his works of art and to entertain his illustrious friends, including the composer George Frideric Handel, the poet Alexander Pope, and the writer Jonathan Swift.

Whig statesman and Foreign Secretary, Charles James Fox died here, as did Prime Minister George Canning.

For many years Chiswick House was the home of successive Dukes of Devonshire, but in 1892 the 8th Duke moved to Chatsworth in Derbyshire and the house became a private mental asylum. Middlesex County Council purchased the building in 1929 and, over the next 30 years, it was sadly allowed to fall into a state of disrepair.

In 1958, the Ministry of Works began an extensive restoration project, aiming to restore the house to its former glory. As the workmen set about their task, they appear to have disturbed the spirits of several former residents. The aroma of bacon and eggs, which the workmen attributed to the ghost of "one of the mad cooks," often wafted around the building, despite the fact that no cooking ever took place in the vicinity.

Although the restoration was completed long ago, staff and visitors are still mystified by the distinctive smell of fried bacon that sometimes permeates the air in the back gallery. It can hang in the air for several months at a time, and then not be noticed for a few years.

Elsewhere in the house, visitors have sensed a female presence in one of the bedrooms. On one occasion, a woman was admiring the mirror in this room— it is the only original mirror in the house— and was startled by the distinctive reflection of Lady Burlington standing behind her. However, when she turned around, the woman found that her spectral companion was nowhere to be seen.

◀ *The ghostly aroma of fried bacon is often smelled at the elegant Chiswick House.*

# ⓘ information

## Contact details

Chiswick House
Burlington Lane
Chiswick
London, W4 2RP

☎ +44 (0)20 8995 0508

www Chiswick House site
www.chgt.org.uk

## Transport links

⊖ Turnham Green

🚆 Chiswick

# NORTH LONDON

Wilderness and bygone ambience are to be found to the north of London. The bracing expanse of Hampstead Heath offers the intrepid seeker of the unknown the opportunity to encounter a galloping horseman, while venturing into the lovely village of Hampstead, you can seek out several historic, though haunted, pubs. Nearby in the village of Highgate, prepare to have your marrow chilled as you wander among the crumbling tombs of the vast necropolis of Highgate Cemetery.

## HAUNTED LOCATIONS

(1) The Flask Tavern

(2) Hampsted Ponds and Heath

(3) Holly Bush

(4) Pond Square

(5) The Spaniards Inn

(6) The Flask

(7) The Gatehouse

(8) Highgate Cemetery

(9) Rose and Crown

(10) Bell Lane

(11) Bruce Castle

# THE FLASK TAVERN
## 14 FLASK WALK, NW3

See map p.123 (1)

##  MONTY KEEPS A WATCHFUL EYE

Tucked away at the end of a pedestrian thoroughfare that leads from Hampstead High Street, The Flask Tavern is very much a pub for locals. Its name recalls the days in the 18th century when Hampstead attempted to reinvent itself as a spa village, and people trekked up from the City of London to take the waters at its Chalybeate Wells. Anxious to capitalize on the passing trade, the landlord of the pub began selling flasks to those visiting the spa, and thus the pub acquired its name.

The ghost of a 19th-century landlord, whom tradition remembers as "Monty," haunts the hostelry. Nobody really knows much about his living self, but in death his revenant likes to keep an eye on those who are now entrusted with the running of his pub. Monty finds change particularly irksome, and he was moved to spectral indignation by the redevelopment of The Flask's conservatory in 1997. He disrupted work as often as he could by hiding the workmen's tools and switching off plugs. Once the building work was complete, the ghostly landlord continued to disturb the pub, frequently interrupting customers' meals by moving tables across the floor in front of them. Recently, however, Monty has become relatively inactive.

*Monty the 19th-century landlord keeps a ghostly eye on The Flask in Hampstead.* ▶

---

## (i) information

### Contact details

The Flask Tavern
14 Flask Walk
Hampstead
London, NW3 1HE

 +44 (0)20 7435 4580

 **The Flask Tavern site**
www.theflaskhampstead.co.uk

flask@youngs.co.uk

### Transport links

⊖ Hampstead

# HAMPSTEAD PONDS AND HEATH

HAMPSTEAD, NW3                 See map p.123

## ☞ THE HORSEMAN'S SHADOW

Hampstead Heath is comprised of 800 acres (325 hectares) of wild and rugged parkland, which as well as being a playground for generations of Londoners, also provides a lush habitat for an abundance of wildlife. Yet in parts, the Heath is a sinister place, with towering trees casting its rough pathways into ethereal shadow. Numerous ponds dot the Heath and some of these are used by hardy swimmers, who sometimes complain of hearing phantom footsteps following them along the jetties as they prepare to leap into the cold, murky waters. No explanation has ever been found as to who—or what—might be responsible for the footsteps, although several witnesses believe them to be the ghosts of those who have committed suicide in the ponds.

During the 17th and 18th centuries, the rugged paths that cross the Heath's untamed wilderness were the haunt of numerous highwaymen, the so-called "Gentlemen of the Road," who would stop at nothing to relieve travelers of their possessions and even their lives. The wide open spaces of the Heath afford travelers little protection, making them easy prey for criminals.

It would seem that one such felon found the lure of the Heath so irresistible that he is loath to leave it. Over the years, there have been numerous reports of a dark figure on horseback, which comes riding from the dense thickets and gallops toward astonished witnesses. One woman who encountered the phantom told how she was so convinced that she was about to be trampled to death that she flung herself to the ground and prepared for the impact. After a few moments, she looked up to find that the ghostly rider and his mount had apparently vanished into thin air. Only then did it dawn on her that, despite the fact that they were coming toward her at great speed, the horse's hooves had not made the slightest sound upon the hard ground.

 *Those who swim in the waters of Hampstead Ponds speak of chilling footsteps following them on the jetties.*

## ⓘ information

### Contact details

Hampstead Heath
Hampstead
London, NW5 1QR

💻 **Hampstead Heath site**
www.hampsteadheath.net

### Transport links

⊖ Hampstead Heath;
Hampstead; Kentish Town

**128**

# HOLLY BUSH
## HOLLY MOUNT, NW3

See map p.123

## ☞ THE PHANTOM WAITRESS

If you have lunch in the gas-lit, 18th-century Holly Bush inn and find your order being taken by a polite waitress, wearing a white linen apron over a long, dark skirt, do not be surprised if your meal never arrives.

"We don't offer waitress service," says Peter Dures, who, with his wife Hazel, ran the pub during the mid-1990s, would explain wearily to irate customers who had stormed up to the bar demanding to know why their meals were taking so long. "But we gave our order to a waitress," these patrons insisted invariably. "Then I'm sorry," Peter would reply, "but you've given your order to our ghost!" Nobody knows who she was or is, and nobody knows why she has this compunction to come back and wait on tables in death. But come back she does, and no one can fault her, as she is extremely courteous as she takes an order. The one thing she doesn't do, however, is to deliver your order to the kitchen so that your meal can be prepared!

In the late 1950s, a resident jazz band used to perform at the Holly Bush on Sunday nights. The bandleader always finished his set by walking off the tiny dais on which he had been performing and slapping the pianist on the back as he walked past. Peter and Hazel resurrected the inn's musical tradition, only to find that their piano player was often rewarded with a phantom slap on his back.

## ⓘ information

### Contact details

Holly Bush
22 Holly Mount
London, NW3 6SG

☎ +44 (0)20 7435 2892

 **Pub guide site**
www.beerintheevening.com
/pubs/s/35/3569/Holly_Bush
/Hampstead

### Transport links

 Hampstead

 Finchley Road & Frognal

# POND SQUARE

HIGHGATE, N6

See map p.123 (4)

## ☞ THE GHOSTLY CHICKEN

Sir Francis Bacon was a politician, writer, and philosopher who also liked to dabble in scientific experiments. He was one of the first people to propagate the theory that refrigeration might be utilized as a means of preserving meat and in January 1926, on a bitterly cold morning, he decided to put his theory to the test. Having purchased a chicken from an old woman on Highgate Hill he slaughtered and plucked the bird and stuffed its carcass with snow.

By a deliciously ironic twist of fate, Sir Francis caught a severe chill as a result of his experiment and was taken to nearby Arundel House, where he died shortly afterward.

Ever since Bacon's death, there have been frequent reports of a phantom white bird, resembling a plucked chicken, which appears from nowhere to race round Pond Square in frenzied circles, flapping its wings as it runs.

In 1943, a man named Terence Long was crossing the square late at night when he heard a raucous shriek and the ghostly chicken appeared before him. It proceeded to race around frantically, before vanishing into thin air.

In the 1970s, a courting couple were interrupted when the chicken dropped suddenly from above and landed next to them!

In recent years, however, sightings of the featherless phantom have been few and far between.

---

## ⓘ information

**Contact details**

Pond Square
Highgate
London, N6

**Transport links**

⊖ Highgate

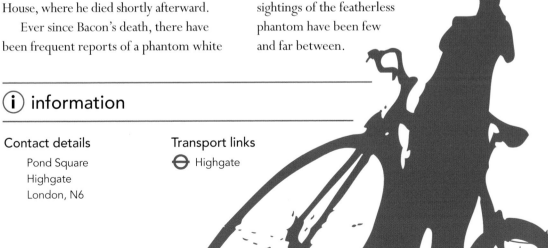

# THE SPANIARDS INN

**SPANIARDS ROAD, NW3**

See map p.123 **(5)**

##  TURPIN'S COSY LAIR

The 16th-century Spaniards Inn stands on the edge of Hampstead Heath and is as pleasant a hostelry as you could ever wish to encounter. It is a low-beamed, atmospheric old place, reputedly named after two Spanish brothers who both fell in love with the same woman and then killed each other in a duel.

During the Gordon Riots of 1780, the rioters stopped off at the inn on their way to destroy nearby Kenwood House, which was then the home of the unpopular Earl of Mansfield. The quick-witted landlord assured the rioters of his loyalty to their cause and to demonstrate his solidarity offered them unlimited refreshments. Thus was he able to stall them until military aid arrived and the destruction of Kenwood was prevented.

The Inn was also a favored haunt of highwayman Dick Turpin, who is commemorated by the snug Turpin Bar on the second floor, where a warming log fire crackles in an ancient hearth in the winter months. Customers enjoying a quiet pint in this particular room have experienced the mysterious sensation of having their sleeves tugged by an invisible hand. In the downstairs bar, meanwhile, a shadowy cloaked figure—who some believe to be Turpin himself—has been known to stride purposefully across the bar before vanishing abruptly into the wall near the toilets.

◀ *The Spaniards Inn is one of the many pubs to claim Dick Turpin's ghost as an ethereal regular.*

## ⓘ information

### Contact details

The Spaniards Inn
Spaniards Road
London, NW3 7JJ

 +44 (0)20 8731 8406

 **The Spaniards Inn site**
www.thespaniardshampstead.co.uk

### Transport links

 Hampstead

**132**

# THE FLASK
## HIGHGATE WEST HILL, N6

See map p.123 ⑥

##  THE BULLET IN THE WALL

The 18th-century Flask is one of Highgate's most atmospheric pubs, which is believed to have been patronized by highwayman Dick Turpin and the artist William Hogarth. It is said that Hogarth once produced an instant sketch of a fight that he witnessed on the premises between two customers who set about each other with their beer tankards.

The ghost of a female phantom haunts the pub, although nobody is certain of her identity. Some claim that she is the ghost of one of the pub's former maidservants, who committed suicide when an illicit romance turned sour. Others maintain that her apparition is connected with a bullet that is embedded in the wall of the snug bar to the right of the entrance. Nobody is certain when, why, or at whom the bullet was fired and its link to the haunting is somewhat tenuous, to say the least.

However, the staff know when her ghost is about to honor them with a visit, because her appearances are presaged by a sudden and alarming drop in temperature, even on a hot summer's day. A full-blown manifestation is a rare occurrence, but lights certainly begin to sway back and forth mysteriously, glasses are moved across tables in front of surprised customers, and some people even suffer the alarming sensation of feeling her invisible form blowing gently down the backs of their necks.

---

## ⓘ information

### Contact details

The Flask
77 Highgate West Hill
London, N6 6BU

 +44 (0)20 8348 7346

 **Pub guide site**
www.beerintheevening.com
/pubs/s/51/5199/Flask
/Highgate

### Transport links

🚇 Highgate

# THE GATEHOUSE

NORTH ROAD, N6

See map p.123 (7)

##  THE GHOST OF MOTHER MARNES

This rambling pub, which was rebuilt in 1905, is named after the gateway at which travelers once paid their tolls to cross land owned by the Bishop of London.

Several ghosts are believed to haunt The Gatehouse. The best known is that of Mother Marnes, an old woman who was murdered in the original gatehouse for her meager life savings. One night in the 1960s, the landlord of the time went up to the minstrels' gallery and was attacked by "something" that came at him from the shadows. "I had gone up to switch off the gallery lights," he recalled, "when all of a sudden this thing appeared from nowhere. I can remember nothing else until waking up in hospital." However, no sooner had the landlord recovered and returned to the pub, than he was attacked by the entity again. He was so terrified that he requested a transfer.

The minstrels' gallery has since been converted into a pub theater. When landlord John Plews and his staff cleared out the room, they threw out years of accumulated junk, with the exception of a heavy table, which they left in the center of the room. On several occasions, John and his staff unlocked the door in the mornings to find that the table had been mysteriously placed under the window during the night. Despite a thorough investigation, John never discovered any logical reason for the table's movement, and concluded that it must have been the ghost enjoying a spectral prank.

## (i) information

### Contact details

The Gatehouse
1 North Road
London, N6 4BD

 +44 (0)20 8340 8054

 Pub guide site
www.beerintheevening.com
/pubs/s/33/3310
/Gatehouse/Highgate

### Transport links

 Highgate

## 134 HIGHGATE CEMETERY
SWAIN'S LANE, N6

See map p.123 (8)

##  THE CITY OF THE DEAD

Sprawling across 20 acres (8 hectares) of grassy hillside, Highgate Cemetery opened in 1839, and quickly became the most sought-after burial ground in London. Many famous and illustrious names have been laid to rest in its hallowed ground. However, as the dark days of World War II descended upon the capital, the cemetery's fortunes suffered a downturn and by the 1960s this once-proud necropolis had been abandoned.

Rumors were soon circulating of sinister cults holding strange ceremonies in the abandoned ruins after dark. Then, the local newspaper, the *Hampstead and Highgate Express*, began to receive letters from frightened readers telling of ghostly encounters around the cemetery.

One man, whose car had broken down nearby, was terrified by a hideous apparition with glowing red eyes, glaring at him through the rusting iron gates. Another man walking along the dark and foreboding Swain's Lane, found himself suddenly knocked to the ground by a fearsome creature that "seemed to glide" from the wall of the cemetery. He was only saved from the monster when the headlights of an approaching car seemed to cause the thing to dissolve into thin air.

When it was subsequently suggested that a vampire might be loose in the old cemetery the hunt for the undead was underway, as a barrage of journalists, camera crews, and eager occultists swarmed around the grim, decaying mausoleums.

Meanwhile, letters telling of frightening encounters in the vicinity of Swain's Lane continued to grace the pages of the local press. A ghostly cyclist, puffing his way up the steep incline had terrified one young mother, while other unfortunate locals had witnessed a tall man in a top hat, strolling nonchalantly across the road before disappearing into the wall of the cemetery.

In the 1980s, a massive restoration project by the Friends of Highgate Cemetery went some way to reversing the neglect of the previous decades. As they cleared the pathways and uncovered many of the spectacular tombs, the ghostly activity began to recede. Today, spectral sightings are reduced to just two figures. One is the

 Over the years, Highgate Cemetery has played host to a series of hauntings.

ghost of a mad old woman, her long gray hair streaming behind her as she races among the graves, searching for her children, whom she is supposed to have murdered in a fit of insane rage. The other is a shrouded figure who gazes pensively into space, seemingly oblivious to the presence of witnesses, until they get too close, whereupon it vanishes.

## ⓘ information

### Contact details

Highgate Cemetry
Swain's Lane
Highgate
London, N6 6PJ

 +44 (0)20 8340 1834

💻 Highgate Cemetery site
www.highgate-cemetery.org

info@highgate-cemetery.org

### Transport links

Ⓣ Archway; Highgate

# ROSE AND CROWN
## CLAY HILL, EN2

See map p.123 **9**

##  TURPIN KEEPS ON RIDING

The ghost of the notorious 18th-century highwayman Dick Turpin must be one of the busiest in England! For that matter, with the number of pubs that claim his living self as a regular, it is a miracle he was ever able to remain upright in the saddle.

Turpin's grandfather, one Mr. Mott, was once the proprietor of the Rose and Crown and local tradition maintains that the highwayman often hid at the pub in order to evade capture. His ghost is said to haunt not only the pub but also the road outside, where Turpin gallops hell for leather through the night astride a jet black mount, no doubt en route to one of the many other pubs he is obliged to haunt before daybreak!

## ⓘ information

### Contact details

Rose and Crown
185 Clay Hill
Enfield, EN2 9AJ

 +44 (0)20 8366 0864

www Pub guide site
www.beerintheevening.
com/pubs/s/32/32854/
Rose_and_Crown/Enfield

### Transport links

 Gordon Hill

# BELL LANE
ENFIELD, EN3

See map p.123 (10)

##  THE ENFIELD FLYER

On a crisp December evening in 1961, young Robert Bird was cycling along Bell Lane on his way to a Boys' Brigade meeting, when he saw a pair of lights speeding toward him. As the lights came closer they suddenly swerved across the road and seemed to be heading straight toward him.

Convinced that an out-of-control vehicle was about to run him over, Robert attempted to move out of its path. But it was too late, and he braced himself for the inevitable impact. But the whole scene suddenly seemed to progress in slow motion, and Robert was able to observe that the vehicle was actually a black coach being pulled by four horses, all spurred on by two shadowy figures. Strangest of all was the fact that the carriage was actually traveling several feet off the ground. Then, just as the coach was about to hit the boy, it passed straight through him and vanished.

This was probably the "Phantom Coach of Enfield," a ghostly conveyance that races along Bell Lane with its wheels suspended above the ground. Legend has it that its origins lie in the 18th century, when the countryside in this area consisted of marshland, and the road was a lot higher than it is today. It was quite common at the time for speeding coaches to veer from the highway and plunge headlong into the swampy surroundings, often with tragic results. Is it possible that this ghostly coach is a vestige of such a tragedy?

---

## (i) information

### Contact details

Bell Lane
Enfield
Middlesex, EN3

### Transport links

 Turkey Street;
Enfield Lock

**38**

# BRUCE CASTLE
## LORDSHIP LANE, N17

See map p.123 (11)

## ☞ THE MELANCHOLIC SHADE OF LADY COLERAINE

This Tudor manor house was once the home of postal reformer Sir Rowland Hill and is believed to stand on the site of a castle built by Scottish king Robert the Bruce's father.

For many years, Bruce Castle was owned by the Coleraine family and it is the ghost of the wife of the 2nd Lord Coleraine, which is said the haunt the building.

Above the clock on the exterior of Bruce Castle, a small window can be seen and it was in this room that the 2nd Lord Coleraine is said to have imprisoned his beautiful wife, Constantia, for fear that anyone else should gaze upon her. Distraught at her detention, the poor woman was finally overcome by grief, and on November 3, 1680, Constantia leaped to her death from the balustrade, with her baby in her arms.

Her disturbing screams echoed down the centuries, and were heard on the anniversary of her death each year. However, in the early 20th century, a sympathetic clergyman took pity on her agonized spirit and held a prayer service in her room in the hope of laying it to rest. Although he managed to quell the woman's screams, her silent shade occasionally repeats her suicide.

In July 1971, two people walking past the building late one night noticed a group of revelers in 18th-century costume, who were apparently enjoying a ball. What caught their attention was the fact that these strangely attired guests were making no sound and appeared to be floating in mid-air. A few days later, another couple saw the same mysterious figures and approached them to enquire what was happening, whereupon the figures slowly melted into thin air …

▼ *The agonized spirit of Lord Coleraine's wife sometimes appears at Bruce Castle.*

# ⓘ information

## Contact details

Bruce Castle Museum
Lordship Lane
London, N17 8NU

 +44 (0)20 8808 8772

 Bruce Castle Museum site
www.haringey.gov.uk/leisure
/brucecastlemuseum.htm

museum.services@haringey.gov.uk

## Transport links

 Seven Sisters;
Wood Green

 Bruce Grove

# EAST LONDON

The east of London might not be as overrun with ghosts as other parts of the capital, but the locations where they choose to appear are certainly impressive and historic. Hackney's Sutton House is a place of creaking floorboards and shadowy corners, and Commercial Street's Ten Bells pub has changed little since the Jack-the-Ripper murders held the surrounding neighborhood in a grip of steely terror.

## HAUNTED LOCATIONS

1. The Ten Bells
2. The Bow Bells
3. St Mary the Virgin
4. Sutton House
5. The George
6. Chingford Mount Cemetery

**142**

# THE TEN BELLS
## COMMERCIAL STREET, E1

See map p.141 (1)

##  JACK THE RIPPER'S LOCAL

The interior of The Ten Bells pub, resplendent with a magnificent tiled wall panel depicting the days when this area was countryside outside the City of London, has hardly changed since the 19th century.

It was in the early hours of November 9, 1888, when Mary Kelly, Jack the Ripper's final victim, left the pub. Her horrifically mutilated body was discovered the next morning in Miller's Court, off Dorset Street on the opposite side of the road from The Ten Bells. Indeed, for many years in the 1970s and 1980s, the pub was renamed The Jack The Ripper, until, thanks largely to a landlord who was tastefully selling dark red "Ripper Tipples," the brewery decided to return it to its original name in 1989.

In the late 1990s live-in staff, whose bedrooms were on the upper floors of the building, began to complain of alarming encounters with a ghostly old man dressed in Victorian clothing. They were often awoken by an uneasy feeling in the dead of night, and would find his phantom form lying beside them on the bed! As soon as they cried out in shock, the figure disappeared. Staff with no previous knowledge of his ghost would often report seeing him, and their descriptions would always be the same. Nobody had any idea who he was and those who had occasion to live on the premises learned to accept him as the pub's oldest resident.

In June 2000, a new landlord took over the pub and decided to clear out the cellar. He found an old metal box hidden away in a corner, and on opening it, discovered that it contained the personal effects of a man named George Roberts. The items dated from the early 1900s and with them was a brown leather wallet, inside which was a press cutting from the same period that talked of his having been murdered with an ax in a Swansea movie theater. Research revealed that a man named George Roberts had kept the pub in the late 19th and early 20th centuries and the landlord concluded that it was his ghost whom staff had been encountering.

▲ *The wraith at The Ten Bells pub may well be the ghost of an ex-landlord.*

## (i) information

### Contact details

The Ten Bells
84 Commercial Street
London, E1 6LY

☎ +44 (0)20 7366 1721

 **Pub guide site**

www.beerintheevening.com
/pubs/s/24/2425
/Ten_Bells/Shoreditch

### Transport links

⊖ Aldgate East; Aldgate

 Liverpool Street;
Shoreditch High Street

144

# THE BOW BELLS
## BOW ROAD, E3

See map p.141 (2)

## ☞ FLUSHED BY THE GHOST

▲ The ghost of The Bow Bells refuses to leave the ladies' bathroom.

The Bow Bells pub stands on Mile End Road and has a down-at-heel ambience about it. Its ghost has the annoying—not to say alarming—habit of flushing the lavatory in the ladies' bathroom as patrons happen to be sitting on it!

In 1974, in a determined attempt to be rid of the phantom responsible, the landlord decided to hold a séance. As the sitters gathered around and asked the spirit to make itself known, the bathroom door suddenly swung open with such violence that a pane of its glass was shattered. Since then, successive landlords have grown used to sharing their pub with their lavatory-flushing guest.

## (i) information

### Contact details

The Bow Bells
116 Bow Road
London, E3 3AA

☎ +44 (0)20 8981 7317

### Pub guide site

www.beerintheevening.com
/pubs/s/52/5275
/Bow_Bells/Bow

### Transport links

⊖ Bow Road;
Bow Church DLR

# ST MARY THE VIRGIN
### OVERTON DRIVE, E11

See map p.141 **3**

**145**

##  REUNITED AFTER ALL THESE YEARS

A startling though poignant haunting has reputedly been witnessed in the churchyard that surrounds the 18th-century St Mary's Church. A skeleton, its bones bleached white, is said to cross the churchyard wheeling a coffin cart. As it approaches one of the tombs, a spectral wraith in a white shroud is said to rise from the earth and the two proceed to embrace one another. Witnesses, however, have nothing to fear, for the two are said to be a husband and wife who, for reasons unknown, were buried in separate parts of the churchyard and now enjoy occasional ghostly reunions before amazed spectators.

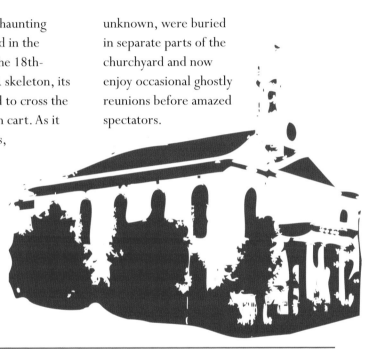

## (i) information

### Contact details

St Mary the Virgin
Overton Drive
Wanstead
London, E11 2LW

 +44 (0)20 8989 9101

www **St Mary The Virgin site**
www.parishofwanstead.org

### Transport links
⊖ Wanstead; Snaresbrook

**146**

# SUTTON HOUSE
## HOMERTON HIGH STREET, E9

See map p.141 ④

## ☞ HOWLING HOUNDS AND SHIMMERING WRAITHS

The splendid red-brick Sutton House was built in 1535 by Sir Ralph Sadleir, one of Henry VIII's Privy Councillors. Since then it has been home to Huguenot silk weavers, Victorian schoolmistresses, and Edwardian clergy. By the 1980s, the building had fallen

▼ *Sutton House is one of London's oldest and most haunted mansions.*

into disrepair, its decline aided by squatters and vandals. Thankfully, largely due to the efforts of the Sutton House Community Scheme, the building was restored in the early 1990s and is now open to the public under the auspices of the National Trust. Although it has altered over the years, it remains essentially a Tudor house and its oak-panelled walls, grand staircase, and carved fireplaces are reminiscent of a bygone age.

Several ghosts wander its atmospheric interior, including those of dogs that can be heard wailing from the empty house in the dead of night. They are thought to be the pets of John Machell, a wealthy wool merchant who lived at Sutton House from 1550 to 1558. Images of the hounds can still be seen in the coat of arms in the fireplace of the building's Little Chamber.

Whenever dogs are brought into Sutton House today, they often stop rigid at the foot of the staircase, their hackles raised, apparently transfixed by something they can see on the stairs but which remains invisible to humans.

Another ghost of the house is that of the White Lady, thought to be Frances, the wife of John Machell the Younger. She died giving birth to twins on May 11, 1574 and her shimmering shade has been seen gliding around the building.

During the renovation of the property in the 1990s, an architectural student staying at the house woke up in what is now the exhibition room to find a lady in a blue dress hovering over his bed. A house steward recently encountered this same specter when she interrupted his slumbers by violently shaking his bed in the night.

Sudden drops in temperature, doors that open of their own accord, and objects flung across rooms are just some of the other phenomena to be regularly encountered at this atmospheric old time capsule.

## (i) information

### Contact details

Sutton House
2 & 4 Homerton High Street
Hackney
London, E9 6JQ

 +44 (0)20 8986 2264

 National Trust site
www.nationaltrust.org.uk
/main/w-suttonhouse

### Transport links

 Hackney Central;
Hackney Downs

# THE GEORGE

## HIGH STREET, E11

See map p.141

##  MAD MOLLIE

A murder committed long ago and its tragic aftermath have apparently left their ethereal mark on the fabric of this otherwise pleasant Wanstead pub. The ghost is said to be that of "Mad Mollie" a 19th-century barmaid who is believed to have thrown her illegitimate child onto the pub's fire and then hanged herself from an upstairs beam.

Although her body was cut down, it disappeared soon afterward, and its whereabouts have never been discovered. Her remorseful wraith sometimes returns to wander the bar of the pub; a trapped entity doomed to contemplate her evil deed for the whole of eternity.

 *The ghost of "Mad Mollie" roams the bar of The George public house.*

---

## (i) information

### Contact details

The George
159 High Street
Wanstead
London, E11 2RL

 +44 (0)20 8989 2921

**Pub guide site**

www.beerintheevening.com/pubs/s/24/2430/George/Wanstead

### Transport links

⊖ Wanstead

# CHINGFORD MOUNT CEMETERY

OLD CHURCH ROAD, E4

See map p.141 (6)

##  THE HORSEMAN COMETH

This vast necropolis, consisting mostly of Victorian graves, was once part of the estate of Lady Hamilton, the famed lover of British naval commander Horatio Nelson. Among its later occupants were the infamous Kray twins, Ronnie and Reggie.

In 1971, the cemetery's superintendent reported that he and his wife had frequently been disturbed by "eerie voices, whining noises and shaking sounds" in the dead of night. His son even witnessed a cloaked figure on a black horse cantering over the grass.

More recently two women walking past the cemetery gates, heard voices whispering in conspiratorial tones, although there was nobody else around at the time.

---

##  information

---

### Contact details

Chingford Mount Cemetery
121 Old Church Road
London, E4 6ST

 +44 (0)20 8524 5030

 **Waltham Forest Council site**
www.walthamforest.gov.uk
/index/environment
/funerals/cemeteries
/chingford-mount-cemetery.htm

john.billson@walthamforest.gov.uk

### Transport links

🚆 Highams Park

# SOUTHEAST LONDON

This varied chapter will take you to some truly mysterious places. Step into the charming George Inn, which is haunted by the ghost of a landlady who attempts to keep the contemporary world firmly at bay and head down the river Thames to find a rich array of haunted buildings in the village of Greenwich.

## HAUNTED LOCATIONS

(1) The Old Vic

(2) Elephant and Castle Underground

(3) Old Operating Theatre

(4) The Anchor

(5) The London Dungeon

(6) University of Greenwich

(7) Trafalgar Tavern

(8) The George Inn

(9) The Queen's House

(10) Hare and Billet Road

(11) Cutty Sark

(12) Blackwall Tunnel

(13) The O2

(14) Charlton House

(15) Lesnes Abbey Woods

(16) Horniman Museum

(17) Hall Place

(18) The Old Palace

**152**

# THE OLD VIC
## THE CUT, SE1

See map p.151

### ☞ THE BLOODSTAINED SPECTER

Dating from the early part of the 19th century, and originally known as the Royal Coburg Theatre, The Old Vic was renamed the Royal Victoria Theatre in 1833, in honor of the young Princess Victoria. In 1912, Lillian Baylis became its manager and set about raising its standards. She was so successful that by the end of World War I, it had become one of London's leading theaters.

▼ *The spectral actress at The Old Vic appears with bloodstained hands.*

Over the years, there have been several reports from startled witnesses of a spectral woman who has been seen in various parts of the theater clasping her bloodstained hands to her breast. It is believed, but by no means proven, that the blood is actually make up and that the revenant is an actress from a Shakespearean tragedy performed long ago. Unwilling to take a final bow, this ghost feels compelled to repeat her ghostly encore over and over again.

---

## ⓘ information

**Contact details**

The Old Vic, 103 The Cut
London, SE1 8NB

 **The Old Vic site**
www.oldvictheatre.com

☎ 0844 871 7628 (UK)
+44 (0)20 7928 2651 (non UK)

ovtcadmin@oldvictheatre.com

**Transport links**

 Southwark;
Lambeth North; Waterloo

 Waterloo

# ELEPHANT AND CASTLE UNDERGROUND

## LONDON ROAD, SE1

See map p.151 ②

### THE PASSENGER WHO NEVER LEAVES

Ghostly footsteps are often heard running through Elephant and Castle Underground station on storm-tossed winter nights. Nobody knows what lies behind the phenomenon, but it has chilled the blood of many maintenance workers employed at the station during the night.

A ghostly young woman in dark clothing has also been observed boarding trains at the station and walking through the carriages, however, she has always disappeared by the time the train pulls into the next station.

## (i) information

### Contact details

Elephant and Castle
Underground
London Road
Elephant and Castle
London, SE1 6LW

 +44 (0)20 7222 1234

 **London Town site**
www.londontown.com
/LondonInformation
/Underground_Stations
/Elephant__Castle/ee84/

### Transport links

 Elephant and Castle

154

# OLD OPERATING THEATRE

ST THOMAS STREET, SE1 See map p.151

##  PHANTOM FLORENCE

The Old Operating Theatre is without doubt one of London's most atmospheric and unique locations. It is situated in a church roof and reached via a winding, wooden staircase that clings precariously to a wall. Once used as the herb garret for nearby St Thomas's Hospital, it became its female operating theater in 1822 and remained so until 1862 when it was sealed up and forgotten. It was restored in 1956 and now functions as a medical museum.

It is also hired out for private parties at night, and staff working at these have come to terms with the fact that the place is haunted. Phantom footsteps have been heard running up the wooden staircase toward the storeroom, although when witnesses go to investigate there is never anyone there.

It was at St Thomas's Hospital that famed British nurse Florence Nightingale founded her school of nursing in 1860, and some think she might be one of the spirits that haunt the Old Operating Theatre.

A photograph that had been taken of the museum interior was once displayed on the wall, and many people claimed that they could see the apparition of a ghostly nurse standing in the background. Indeed, several people went so far as to insist that the image was unmistakably that of Florence Nightingale herself.

*Florence Nightingale may be one of the ghosts that haunt the Old Operating Theatre.*

---

## (i) information

### Contact details

Old Operating Theatre
9a St Thomas Street
London, SE1 9RY

 +44 (0)20 7188 2679

www Old Operating Theatre site
www.thegarret.org.uk

curator@thegarret.org.uk

### Transport links

⊖ London Bridge

# THE ANCHOR
## PARK STREET, SE1

See map p.151

## ☞ THE MANGY OLD DOG WALKS AGAIN

Situated across the Thames from St Paul's Cathedral, this rambling 18th-century tavern was once a favorite watering hole of the writer Samuel Johnson. It was also an infamous haunt of smugglers, who would hide their ill-gotten contraband in the secret rooms and cubbyholes with which the pub is riddled.

Here too came the notorious press gangs, to cajole, bribe, or even abduct "volunteers" to crew the ships that sailed from the busy river port that London once was. Legend tells of one unfortunate conscript who put up a great resistance as a gang tried to drag him, kicking and screaming, from the pub one night. The other customers, who averted their eyes and gazed into their tankards rather than risk attracting the attentions of the pressmen to themselves, politely ignored his cries. The man's dog, however, attempted a spirited defense of his master and barked and snapped at the kidnappers, until one of the gang slammed the door shut with such force that it caught the animal's tail and cut it clean off. The dog howled in pain and ran off into the night, never to be seen again.

Occasionally, as the clock ticks toward midnight, the sound of a dog's paws padding along the corridors can be heard, and some staff claim to have seen the dejected shade of a mangy mutt wandering the pub, searching —so legend claims—for its severed tail!

---

## ⓘ information

### Contact details

The Anchor
34 Park Street
Bankside, Southwark
London, SE1 9EF

 www Pub guide site
www.beerintheevening.com
/pubs/s/16/1638
/Anchor/Southwark

### Transport links

 ⊖ London Bridge;
Cannon Street; Bank DLR

 ☎ +44 (0)20 7407 1577

# THE LONDON DUNGEON
## TOOLEY STREET, SE1

See map p.151

##  A GHOSTLY ASSAULT

In 1998, psychic investigator Paul Southcott, director of investigations for the grand-sounding "Ufology and Supernatural Society," opted to spend a night in the London Dungeon armed with a video camera. He was determined to investigate reports that the place was haunted and discovered it to be "teeming" with ghosts.

Among the images that he caught on film were five ghostly faces that appeared through a brick wall, a spectral figure floating above the ground, and a human skeleton in a gibbet cage that miraculously, and suddenly, began "growing" flesh. "The Jack the Ripper exhibits and the Judgement Day boat ride … were awash with paranormal activity" he decreed.

Paul also discovered that at least one of the dungeon's specters was not at all friendly. "I was slapped in the face by a ghost in there," he later told the BBC World Service. "It stung initially, then I felt sick and drained for days and suffered headaches."

Although the London Dungeon only moved to the site in 1975, the dank railway arches in which it is located date back to the 19th century. "It's reported that part of the dungeon was once used as a prison" explained Peter Armstrong the manager, "and in the Second World War the arches were even employed as air-raid shelters." Although Peter conceded that many of his staff believed the site to be haunted, he confessed to a healthy scepticism about the claims.

## (i) information

**Contact details**

The London Dungeon
28–34 Tooley Street
London, SE1 2SZ

 +44 (0)20 7403 7221

 **The London Dungeon site**
www.the-dungeons.co.uk
/london/en/index.htm

**Transport links**

 London Bridge; Bank DLR

# UNIVERSITY OF GREENWICH

**CUTTY SARK GARDENS, SE10**

See map p.151  **6**

See map p.151

## ☞ QUEEN BESS & THE MELANCHOLIC ADMIRAL

Formerly the Old Royal Navy College, the buildings that now house the University of Greenwich date from the 17th century and stand on the site of Greenwich Palace. The palace was a favorite residence of Elizabeth I and her ghost returns from time to time. She wears a red wig and a low-necked period dress, but it is the crown that adorns her hairpiece that makes her recognizable.

Admiral John Byng also haunts the college, in the Queen Anne block where he was confined prior to his execution for neglect of duty. His footsteps are heard pacing in the room in which he was imprisoned and he often appears as an apparition. He was last seen on the June 15, 1993, when a security guard saw him walk up the stairs of the Admiral President's block.

## ⓘ information

### Contact details

 University of Greenwich
2 Cutty Sark Gardens
Greenwich
London, SE10 9LW

☎ +44 (0)20 8269 4747

www Old Royal Naval College site
www.oldroyalnavalcollege.org

info@greenwichfoundation.org.uk

### Transport links

 Cutty Sark DLR;
Greenwich DLR

# TRAFALGAR TAVERN

PARK ROW, SE10

See map p.151

## ☞ THE GHOSTLY PIANIST

The Trafalgar Tavern was a favorite haunt of the writer Charles Dickens, who came here to enjoy its famous whitebait dinners, which you can still do today—although the tasty little fish no longer come fresh from the river Thames. Staff maintain that there is a definite "presence" at the pub and that a decidedly icy chill sometimes hangs in the air.

Some people have caught glimpses of a figure walking briskly across the upstairs rooms, although when they take a closer look there is nobody there. Other phenomena includes beer crates being lifted into the air by invisible hands in the pub cellar and the figure of a man in Victorian dress who has been seen sitting by the upstairs piano.

## ⓘ information

### Contact details

Trafalgar Tavern
Park Row
Greenwich
London, SE10 9NW

☎ +44 (0)20 8858 2909

 **Trafalgar Tavern site**
www.trafalgartavern.co.uk

### Transport links

⊖ Cutty Sark DLR; Greenwich DLR

🚆 Greenwich

**160**

# THE GEORGE INN
## BOROUGH HIGH STREET, SE1

See map p.151 **8**

## ☞ THE FORMIDABLE PHANTOM OF MISS MURRAY

For centuries, Southwark's Borough High Street was lined with old coaching inns. "Great rambling, queer old places," according to Charles Dickens in *The Pickwick Papers*. Sadly, only one of them, The George Inn, survived the coming of the railways in the 19th century.

The George Inn dates from 1677 and, as you turn into its cobbled courtyard, it is easy to imagine yourself transported to another age. It, therefore, comes as little surprise to learn that this gem from London's past is haunted. Several members of staff residing on the premises have been woken in the early hours of the morning to find the misty form of a woman floating around their rooms. Nobody knows for sure who she is, but a likely contender is Miss Murray, who kept The George for 50 years in the latter half of the 19th century and the early part of the 20th century.

Having watched so much of the property fall victim to the voracious appetite of the new age of horseless transport, Miss Murray's spirit possesses antagonism toward modern technology. New tills can be guaranteed to go wrong and when engineers are called out to repair them they can never find any logical explanation or genuine fault.

*The former landlady, Miss Murray, may be the ghostly woman seen floating around the rooms at the inn.*

## ⓘ information

### Contact details

The George Inn
77 Borough High Street
Southwark
London, SE1 1NH

 +44 (0)20 7407 2056

 **National Trust site**
www.nationaltrust.org.uk
/main/w-georgeinn

georgeinn@nationaltrust.org.uk

### Transport links

 London Bridge

# 162

# THE QUEEN'S HOUSE
## GREENWICH, SE10

See map p.151 (9)

## ☞ GHOSTS ON FILM?

Designed by British architect Inigo Jones for Charles I's wife, Henrietta Maria, the Queen's House was completed in 1635 and is one of Greenwich's most elegant buildings.

▼ *The Queen's House plays host to some mysterious ghostly figures.*

In 1966, the Reverend and Mrs. R. W. Hardy, from White Rock, British Columbia, visited the house and took a photograph of its magnificent Tulip Staircase. When they returned home and developed the film, a shrouded figure was clearly visible on this particular picture. Closer inspection revealed what appeared to be two figures, apparently ascending what had certainly been an empty staircase.

Despite rigorous examination by photographic experts no rational explanation has ever been put forward to account for the presence of the ghostly figures, other than that they must have been there when the picture was taken.

---

## ⓘ information

### Contact details

The Queen's House
Greenwich
London, SE10 9NF

☎ +44 (0)20 8858 4422

 **The Queen's House site**
www.nmm.ac.uk/places
/queens-house

bookings@nmm.ac.uk

### Transport links

 Cutty Sark DLR;
Greenwich DLR

 Greenwich

# HARE AND BILLET ROAD

BLACKHEATH, SE3

See map p.151  See map p.151 (10)

##  SHE AWAITS HER LOVER

A doomed love affair and its tragic consequences are thought to lie behind the specter that walks its doleful path along Hare and Billet Road.

In the latter half of the 19th century, a Greenwich woman of high birth is said to have fallen in love with a married man. One day, he promised her faithfully that he was about to leave his wife and asked his lover to meet him by a great elm that then stood along a bleak and desolate stretch of Black Heath. But he never came, and the disconsolate lady hanged herself from one of the branches of the tree. Since then, her forlorn phantom has been seen on many occasions, pacing fretfully back and forth along Hare and Billet Road, wringing her hands in despair and hoping beyond hope that her fickle lover will one day appear.

## (i) information

### Contact details

Hare and Billet Road
Blackheath
Lewisham
Greater London, SE3

### Transport links

 Blackheath

# CUTTY SARK

## GREENWICH CHURCH STREET, SE10

See map p.151

##  A STORM IN A BOTTLE

Built in 1869, the *Cutty Sark* unfortunately suffered substantial fire damage in 2007 but has been undergoing extensive restoration.

Many tales are told of sailors witnessing phantom ships in the days when the *Cutty Sark*—a clipper ship—plied its trade on the Australian wool route. Whenever they encountered such an apparition, the terrified sailors would scuttle to the figurehead and cower beneath it imploring its protection.

One day a mariner who was new to the ship, whiled away his time by constructing a model of the *Cutty Sark* in a bottle. This antagonized his crewmates who believed that such a recreation would bring about bad luck. Later that day, a terrible storm blew up and whipped the sea into a foaming frenzy. Suddenly, an enormous five-masted schooner appeared out of nowhere and hurtled toward the *Cutty Sark*. The crew rushed to the figurehead and cowered beneath it, waiting for the collision. A huge wave crashed onto the deck and almost capsized the vessel. But when the ship righted itself, the phantom schooner had vanished. The sailors later learned that, at the exact moment when the ghost ship had disappeared, their comrade had flung his model of the ship overboard into the raging ocean.

*Marooned in dry dock at Greenwich, the Cutty Sark is an eerie place to visit.*

## (i) information

### Contact details

Cutty Sark
2 Greenwich Church Street
Greenwich
London, SE10 9BG

 +44 (0)20 8858 2698

**Cutty Sark site**
www.cuttysark.org.uk

enquiries@cuttysark.org.uk

### Transport links

 Cutty Sark DLR;
Greenwich DLR

Greenwich

# BLACKWALL TUNNEL

## GREENWICH, SE10

See map p.151

##  THE PHANTOM HITCHHIKER

Phantom hitchhikers are a popular, though dubious, part of modern international ghost lore. Indeed, their tales follow an established and common pattern that is amply illustrated by this tale from the Blackwall Tunnel.

In October 1972, a motorcyclist stopped to give a lift to a male hitchhiker on the Greenwich approach to the tunnel. The two managed to hold a conversation, during which the man told the driver where he lived. As their conversation was drowned out by the noise of the traffic, the motorcyclist concentrated on the road. On arrival at the other side, he was astonished to find that his passenger had disappeared. Alarmed and mystified he drove through the tunnel a few times but could find no sign of

the stranger. The next day he went round to the address that the man had supplied him with. There he gave his description of the hitchhiker, only to discover that it matched that of a son of the family who had been killed in the tunnel while riding pillion on a motorcycle several years earlier.

## (i) information

### Contact details

Blackwall Tunnel
Greenwich
Greater London, SE10

 Independent guide site
www.greenwich-guide.org.uk
/blackwall.htm

### Transport links

⊖ North Greenwich;
Blackwall DLR

# THE O2
PENINSULA SQUARE, SE10

See map p.151 (13)

##  THE PROPHETIC LAUGHING PHANTOM

The offices of the South Metropolitan Gas Company, which formerly occupied the site of The O2 arena, were long rumored to be haunted. It was widely believed that the bearded phantom, which put in regular appearances to disrupt the working day of the staff by messing up their desks, was that of Sir George Livesey, the company's former chairman. In life, Livesey had been a philanthropic and popular employer who had, among other things, introduced a profit-sharing scheme for his workers. When he died at the ripe old age of 90 years, 7,000 people turned out to pay their last respects at his funeral.

However, his spirit seems to have been loath to depart from the site where he had spent so much of his working life. When the gasworks were closed down, Livesey could often be seen wandering around the derelict buildings. His spectral activity intensified when work began to clear the ground for the construction of the Millennium Dome (now The O2 arena).

On many occasions, builders looked up from their work to find Livesey's distinguished figure watching over them. After a few moments of incredulous gazing, his face would crack into a wide grin and he would let out a peal of chuckling laughter. Spokespeople for the Millennium project confessed that they were completely baffled by what could be causing the specter such great merriment!

---

## (i) information

### Contact details

The O2
Peninsula Square
London, SE10 0DX

 +44 (0)20 8463 2000

 O2 site
www.theo2.co.uk

customerservices@theo2.co.uk

### Transport links

 North Greenwich

# CHARLTON HOUSE

CHARLTON ROAD, SE7                    See map p.151 (**14**)

 **THE AMOROUS SPECTER**

Charlton House was built between 1607 and 1612 for Sir Adam Newton, Dean of Durham and tutor to Prince Henry, son of James I. When Newton died, it passed to his son, Henry, and via successive owners, it came into the possession of the wealthy East India Merchant, Sir William Langhorne.

As Langhorne grew to old age, he became increasingly distressed that he had no children. In 1715, after his first wife died, he took a second bride who was just 17, undeterred by the fact that he was in his 80s. However, by the time he died two months later, his young wife had been unable to conceive.

Langhorne has proved unwilling to depart from the house, and his determination to beget an heir has continued beyond the grave. His lustful ghost roams the corridors of Charlton House in search of living ladies that take his fancy.

In the past, many women staying at the house were awoken by the alarming sound of their bedroom door handles turning in the dead of night. Those who investigated would open the door only to find the corridor empty. Occasionally women walking down the stairs have had their bottoms pinched by Langhorne's amorous, though invisible, fingers.

◀ *The amorous ghost at Charlton House still seems to be intent on begetting an heir.*

## (i) information

**Contact details**

Charlton House
Charlton Road
London, SE7 8RE

 +44 (0)20 8856 3951

 **Greenwich Council site**
www.greenwich.gov.uk
/Greenwich/LeisureCulture
/VenuesForHire/VenuesCharlton.htm

charlton.house@greenwich.gov.uk

**Transport links**

 Charlton

**170**

# LESNES ABBEY WOODS
## BOSTALL HILL, SE2

See map p.151 **15**

##  THE HOODED PHANTOM

Lesnes Abbey was founded in 1178 by Richard de Lucy, chief judiciary officer of England under King Henry II. It was

▼ *The hooded figure that drifts around the woods is likely to be a past resident of the Abbey.*

considered an act of penance for supporting King Henry in the dispute with Archbishop Thomas Becket. The abbey was suppressed by Cardinal Wolsey in 1525, and, having passed through several hands, it came into the possession of Christ's Hospital and was taken over by the London County Council in 1930. Consisting of over 200 acres (80 hectares) of woodland, carpeted in spring by a rich profusion of daffodils and bluebells, Lesnes Abbey now forms one of London's loveliest open spaces. The abbey ruins were excavated in 1909, which may have disturbed the revenant of one of the long-dead monks, for several people have reported catching ethereal glimpses of a hooded figure flitting around the woods, which abruptly vanishes if they look at it full on.

## ⓘ information

### Contact details
Lesnes Abbey Woods
Bostall Hill
London, SE2

www Bexley Council site
www.bexley.gov.uk/index.a
spx?articleid=3906

### Transport links
 Abbey Wood

# HORNIMAN MUSEUM

LONDON ROAD, SE23 See map p.151 (16)

## 👉 THE DANCING PHANTOMS

In the 1860s, Victorian tea trader Frederick Horniman began collecting specimens and artifacts from around the globe with the express intention of bringing the wider world to Forest Hill. To that end, in 1890, he began opening his house to the public three times a week.

In 1898, Horniman's house was demolished and British architect Charles Harrison Townsend constructed a new museum in the Art Nouveau style. The museum opened in 1901 and was granted as a gift to the people of London in perpetuity for their recreation and their enjoyment. The museum is still thriving and is a wonderful place to visit.

Visitors may also have the opportunity of making the acquaintances of the ghostly man and woman that haunt the terrace at the rear of the museum. Nobody knows for certain who they are, although there is a general consensus from witnesses that they are dressed in the fashions of the 1920s. The man's hair is heavily greased back, while the woman's most notable feature is the bright red dress that she wears. They appear to be enjoying a distant garden party or ball, for those who encounter them are emphatic that they are dancing across the terrace, although no music is ever heard. After a few moments, the waltzing wraiths spin their way into the trees and are gone …

---

## (i) information

---

### Contact details

Horniman Museum
100 London Road
Forest Hill
London, SE23 3PQ

 +44 (0)20 8699 1872

 **Horniman Museum site**
www.horniman.ac.uk

enquiry@horniman.ac.uk

### Transport links

 Forest Hill

**172**

# HALL PLACE
## BEXLEY, DA5

See map p.151 **17**

##  THE BLACK PRINCE

This flint and brick Tudor house with 17th-century additions is named after the 13th-century owners of the property, the At-Halls.

In 1356, it was from this house that Edward III's oldest son, the Black Prince, set off to fight in the French campaign. His phantom still appears at the property, although its manifestations are believed to be a bad omen for the fortunes of England. Clad in black armor, his figure is said to have appeared three times prior to British setbacks in World War II.

Hall Place's second ghost is that of Lady Constance At-Hall, who had the misfortune of witnessing her husband, Sir Thomas, being gored to death by a stag in front of her. In her despair, she is said to have flung herself to her death from the building's tower. Her pitiful moans have been heard around the property, and mysterious footsteps, accompanied by a strange tapping, have also been heard in the dead of night. From time to time, a shadowy figure has been seen gazing forlornly from the tower.

In the 1950s, a medium visited the house and established that a servant girl who suffered personal tragedy at the house causes some of the phenomena. Her ghost has since been seen several times in one of the attic bedrooms.

---

## (i) information

### Contact details

Hall Place
Bourne Road
Bexley
Kent, DA5 1PQ

 +44 (0)1322 526574

www Hall Place site
www.hallplace.com

info@hallplace.org.uk

### Transport links

 Bexley

# THE OLD PALACE

CROYDON, CR0

See map p.151 **18**

##  THE WRINGING SPECTER

Now a school, The Old Palace in Croydon was formerly the home of successive Archbishops of Canterbury, the medieval lords of the manor. It was visited by many royal figures, including Henry III, Edward I, Henry IV, Henry VII, Henry VIII, Mary I, and Elizabeth I. James I of Scotland was held prisoner here before he became king in 1406.

The see of Canterbury relinquished ownership of the site in 1758 after nearly 750 years of occupation, and the building later became an orphanage.

It is the ghost of the mother of one of the 19th-century orphans that is said to haunt the building. She appears terribly sad, wringing her hands as she roams the rooms searching for her lost child.

---

##  information

---

### Contact details

The Old Palace
Old Palace Road
Croydon, CR0 1AX

 **The Old Palace site**
www.oldpalace.croydon.sch.uk

☎ +44 (0)20 8688 2027

### Transport links

 East Croydon;
Church Street (tram)

# SOUTHWEST LONDON

Moving to the southwest suburbs of London, haunted sites become a little thin on the ground. But what the buildings here lack in quantity is more than made up for by the quality of the ghosts that wander their shadows. From the wives of Henry VIII that haunt Hampton Court Palace to the ghostly Cavalier that gallops across Richmond Park, the phantoms of this area are among the most illustrious in London.

## HAUNTED LOCATIONS

(1) Barnes Common

(2) Richmond Palace

(3) Richmond Park

(4) Ham House

(5) Wimbledon Common

(6) New Wimbledon Theatre

(7) Hampton Court Palace

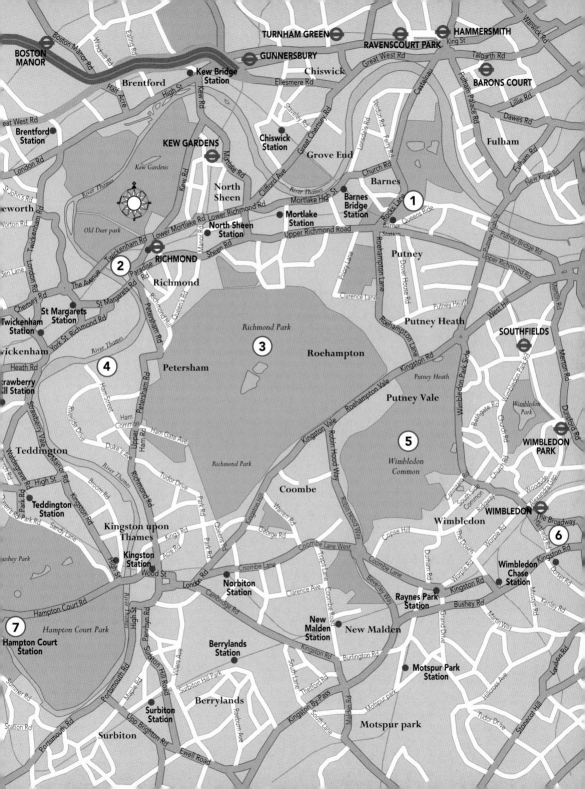

# 176 BARNES COMMON
### COMMON ROAD, SW13

See map p.175 ①

## ☞ THE EXPLOITS OF SPRING HEEL JACK

Little now remains of the original Barnes Common, which in 1838 was one of the haunts of the mysterious and terrifying figure known as "Spring Heel Jack." The spirit would bound toward the common from the vicinity of the old churchyard, his appearance "hideous and frightful … vomiting blue and white flame from his mouth" and attack lone travelers crossing the common at night. However, after a short reign of terror, his appearances came to an end.

Today a man in gray clothes, that some say resemble a prison uniform, is the sole ghostly occupant of Barnes Common. He glides furtively about, looking as though he is about to commit some dastardly crime, but when challenged he melts away before astonished witnesses. One theory is that he is the ghost of a 19th-century convict, who having managed to escape from nearby Putney Hospital, froze to death on the common.

## ⓘ information

### Contact details

Barnes Common
Common Road
London, SW13 9HE

 +44 (0)20 8878 2359

 London Town site

www.londontown.com
/LondonInformation
/Attraction
/Barnes_Common/3219

### Transport links

 Barnes

# RICHMOND PALACE
## OLD PALACE YARD, TW9

##  THE DEATH OF THE VIRGIN QUEEN

Apart from a courtyard and red-brick gatehouse, little now survives of Richmond Palace, but in 1603 it was known as Elizabeth I's "warm winter box."

In January 1603, acting upon the advice of her astrologer, Dr. John Dee, Elizabeth I left Whitehall Palace and headed upriver to Richmond. Shortly after her arrival, she was plunged into depression by word of the death of her cousin and close friend, the Countess of Nottingham. Then, in early March, she came down with a severe chill, which turned into pneumonia. At first, she refused to rest, but by March 21, it was obvious to all that she was close to dying and she finally retired to her bed.

At around 10 pm on the night of March 23, Elizabeth sank into a deep sleep. As she did so, one of her ladies-in-waiting left the room to return briefly to her own quarters. Walking down one of the palace's corridors, she was astonished to meet Elizabeth's figure striding toward her. She looked round to see if anyone else was in the corridor and when she looked back the figure had vanished. Wondering if Elizabeth had made a miraculous recovery, she raced back to the royal bedchamber, but found the monarch still unconscious.

Is it possible that, as the last Tudor monarch clung to life, her spirit had taken a final stroll through Richmond Palace?

## ⓘ information

**Contact details**

Richmond Palace
Old Palace Yard
Richmond
Greater London, TW9

 **Richmond Council site**
www.richmond.gov.uk/local
_history_richmond_palace.pdf

**Transport links**
 Richmond

# RICHMOND PARK
SAWYER'S HILL, TW10 See map p.175 ③

##  THE GHOSTLY CAVALIER

The 2,470 acres (1,000 hectares) that comprise Richmond Park were first enclosed in 1637 by Charles I to enlarge the grounds of Richmond Palace. The park became public property following Charles's execution in 1649, when it was given to the City of London by the Commonwealth government in return for its support during the Civil War. With the Restoration of the monarchy under Charles II, the City returned the land to the Crown.

Today, Richmond Park is a delightful place to wander and take the air, and the profusion of wildlife to which the park is home includes, hares, rabbits, and herds of deer that graze lazily beneath the towering trees. It is also home to a ghost whose origins may well date back to the dark days of the Civil War, when the English population was divided between the Royalists and the Parliamentarians.

In May and June 2003 there were reports of nebulous encounters with a ghostly cavalier amid the foliage of the park. Some people who were walking in the park late in the afternoon spoke of catching fleeting glimpses of this spectral figure. One witness told how he seemed quite solid when spied from afar but spoke of how, as she got closer, he became almost transparent before disappearing into thin air.

*When walking in Richmond Park look out for a ghostly cavalier amid the foliage.*

## ⓘ information

### Contact details
Richmond Park
Sawyer's Hill
Richmond
London, TW10 5

 **Royal Parks site**
www.royalparks.org.uk
/parks/richmond_park/

### Transport links
 Richmond

# HAM HOUSE
HAM, TW10

See map p.175 ④

##  THE SEARCHING SPECTER

Built for Sir Thomas Vavasour in 1610, Ham House was acquired by William Murray, 1st Earl of Dysart, in 1637. In 1651, Murray bequeathed the house to his daughter, Elizabeth, Countess of Dysart, the wife of Sir Lyonel Tollemache. She was also the lover of the Duke of Lauderdale and married him when her husband died in 1672.

An intriguing tale tells of the six-year-old daughter of a 19th-century butler at Ham House who was invited by the then owners, the Ladies Tollemache, to come and stay at the property. In the early hours of the morning, the girl awoke to find a little old lady scratching upon the wall by the fireplace with her fingers. Sitting up to get a better view of the stranger, she seemed to disturb the woman who came to the foot of the bed and proceeded to stare at the child with a fixed and horrible gaze. This sent the child into screaming hysterics, alerting other members of the household who came racing to the room.

They could find no sign of the old woman but, on searching the wall, they uncovered a secret compartment. Within this they uncovered papers that proved that the Countess of Dysart had murdered her first husband in order that she might marry the Duke of Lauderdale.

 *The specter of an old lady has been seen scratching at a wall in Ham House.*

## ⓘ information

**Contact details**

Ham House
Ham
Richmond-upon-Thames
Surrey, TW10 7RS

☎ +44 (0)20 8940 1950

 **National Trust site**
www.nationaltrust.org.uk /main/w-vh/w-visits /w-findaplace/w-hamhouse

hamhouse@nationaltrust.org.uk

**Transport links**
 Richmond

# WIMBLEDON COMMON

WINDMILL ROAD, SW19 See map p.175 (5)

## ☞ WILD AND WINDSWEPT

The 1,100 acres (445 hectares) of Wimbledon Common are desolate in parts and several wanderers have reported encounters with its ghostly inhabitants.

The actor Edward Silward, whom, we are told, was famed in the first half of the 20th century for his "extremely clever impersonation of a gorilla," was crossing the common alone one night, when a man in convict's clothing ran across the ground directly in front of him and promptly disappeared. When discussing the matter with friends, Silward learned that many others had encountered a similar apparition around the common. To this day, people still speak of catching glimpses of a gray figure running across the turf, which has vanished when they attempt to look at it more closely.

In the 18th century, the common was a notorious haunt of footpads (robbers) and highwaymen who were only too willing to relieve travelers of their possessions and even their lives. One of the most infamous was Jerry Abershaw, who was finally brought to justice in 1795. After his execution, his body was hung on a gibbet and placed on Wimbledon Hill to act as a deterrent to others who might be planning similar transgressions. Today his ghost is said to gallop across the common, the dull thud of his phantom mount's hooves clearly audible.

---

## ⓘ information

### Contact details

Wimbledon Common
Windmill Road
Wimbledon
London, SW19 5NR

 +44 (0)20 8788 7655

 **Wimbledon and Putney Commons site**

www.wpcc.org.uk
rangersoffice@wpcc.org.uk

### Transport links

 Wimbledon; Southfields

Wimbledon

# NEW WIMBLEDON THEATRE
THE BROADWAY, SW19

See map p.175 **6**

##  THE CACKLING PHANTOM

The Wimbledon Theatre, as it was formerly known, opened on December 26, 1910, with the pantomime *Jack and Jill*, beginning a tradition of family Christmas shows at the venue that has continued ever since.

The original manager of the theater was the impresario J. B. Mullholland, and his ghostly form has made fleeting returns from time to time to sit in one of the boxes, where he is happy to oversee rehearsals, or to simply watch the play being performed on the stage.

Far more active is "The Gray Lady," who appeared in the bedroom of the manageress in 1980 as just a head and torso. The macabre specter proceeded to ascend to the ceiling, let out a loud, raucous cackle, and vanish. Elsewhere, stagehands and usherettes have seen her misty form, sometimes sitting in the front row of the gallery, and at other times passing through closed doors. On one occasion the ghost was even spotted strolling contentedly out of the ladies' bathroom!

The Gray Lady also has the annoying habit of switching on the theater's sprinkler system. When this last occurred, the safety curtain was quickly lowered to prevent the orchestra pit from flooding. However, staff were most surprised to discover that, although the water had got into the orchestra pit, the safety curtain itself had somehow remained completely dry.

---

## (i) information

### Contact details

New Wimbledon Theatre
93 The Broadway
Wimbledon
London, SW19 1QG

 +44 (0)20 8545 7900

 **Wimbledon Theatre site**
www.ambassadortickets.com
/Wimbledon

### Transport links

 Wimbledon

# HAMPTON COURT PALACE

SURREY, KT8 See map p.175 (7)

## ROYAL REVENANTS

In 1529, Cardinal Wolsey constructed the magnificent Hampton Court Palace on the banks of the Thames. He lived there in regal splendor and offered lavish hospitality to those he entertained until he eventually gave the palace to Henry VIII in an attempt to buy his way back into Royal favor.

Henry wasted no time in introducing his second wife, Anne Boleyn, to the splendors of Wolsey's Palace and, following her beheading in 1536, her ghost remained behind to drift forlornly through its passages and chambers.

Henry's third wife, Jane Seymour, also haunts the Palace, making an annual pilgrimage on the anniversary of her son's birth. Holding an unflickering candle, her head bent in sorrow, she glides eerily along corridors and passes through closed doors.

However, it is Henry's fifth wife Catherine Howard, who makes the most dramatic return to Hampton Court Palace. She was still a teenager when she married the king in 1540 and found him physically repulsive. It wasn't long before she sought

solace in the arms of a young man at court, Thomas Culpeper. Servants' tittle-tattle brought her indiscretions to light and, not long afterward, her adultery was exposed.

Henry was furious at the betrayal and the unfortunate Culpeper was soon languishing in the Tower of London. He was subsequently executed and his unfaithful queen found herself imprisoned in her chambers at Hampton Court.

The young girl decided that her only hope of survival lay in meeting with her husband and pleading with him to spare her life. On November 4, 1541, knowing that Henry would be at prayer in the chapel, she broke free from her guards and ran through what is now known as the "Haunted Gallery" where she threw herself at the chapel's locked door, screaming at her husband to grant her an audience. Henry listened in stony silence and on February 13, 1542, at just 20 years of age, Catherine Howard went bravely to the block with the words: "I die a Queen but I had rather died the simple wife of Tom Culpeper. May God have mercy on my soul. Pray for me."

 *The ghosts of three of Henry VIII's queens vie for your attention at Hampton Court Palace.*

Ever since, servants, noblemen, and even modern-day wardens have reported seeing Catherine's ghost, dressed in a white gown, racing toward the chapel, her face contorted into a terrifying, unearthly scream.

## ⓘ information

### Contact details

Hampton Court Palace
East Molesey
Surrey, KT8 9AU

☎ 0844 482 7777 (UK)
+44 (0)20 3166 6000 (non UK)

 Historic Royal Palaces site

www.hrp.org.uk
/HamptonCourtPalace

hamptoncourt@hrp.org.uk

### Transport links

 Hampton Court

# FURTHER READING

Abbott, Geoffrey *Ghosts of the Tower of London*, Heinemann, 1980

Alexander, Marc *Phantom Britain*, Muller, 1975

Barker, Felix & Silvester-Carr, Denise *The Black Plaque Guide to London*, Constable, 1987

Brooks, J. A *Ghosts of London*, Jarrold, 1993

Byrne, Thomas *Tales From the Past*, Ironmarket, 1977

Coxe, Anthony D. Hippisley, *Haunted Britain*, Pan, 1975

Green, Andrew *Our Haunted Kingdom*, Fontana/Collins, 1973

Hallam, Jack *The Haunted Inns of England*, Wolfe, 1972

Harper, Charles *Haunted Houses*, Bracken, 1993

Jones, Richard *Walking Haunted London*, Interlink, 2007

Jones, Richard *Haunted Britain and Ireland*, New Holland, 2007

Jones, Richard *Myths and Legends of Britain and Ireland*, New Holland, 2012

Jones, Richard *Haunted Castles of Britain and Ireland*, New Holland, 2005

Jones, Richard *Haunted Inns of Britain and Ireland*, New Holland, 2004

Jones, Richard *Walking Dickensian London*, Interlink, 2005

Marsden, Simon, *The Haunted Realm*, Little, Brown, 1986

Mason, John *Haunted Heritage*, Collins and Brown, 1999

McEwan, Graham J. *Haunted Churches of England*, Robert Hale, 1989

Murphy, Ruth & Whicelow, Clive *Mysterious Wimbledon*, Enigma, 1994

Playfair, Guy Lion *The Haunted Pub Guide*, Javelin, 1987

Puttick, Betty *Ghosts of Essex*, Countryside, 1997

Reader's Digest, *Folklore, Myths and Legends of Britain,* Reader's Digest Association Limited, 1977

Underwood, Peter *This Haunted Isle*, Javelin, 1986

Weinrob, Ben & Hibbert, Christopher (editors) *The London Encylopedia*, Macmillan, 1993

# INDEX

# ACKNOWLEDGMENTS

So many people helped with the research and the writing of this book. The staff at the excellent Guildhall Library in London were, as always, a mine of information. The people at various tourist information centers were ever-willing to patiently answer my questions and make useful suggestions. Staff and attendants at the small houses and attractions I visited were always ready with an interesting fact to do with their haunting. Caroline Ryder of the *Highbury and Islington Gazette* was also ready to furnish me with obscure pieces of information. To all of you and those I haven't mentioned I offer my sincere thanks.

At New Holland I'd like to thank Jo Hemmings, Camilla MacWhannell, and Alan Marshall. Karen Arcay and Lindsay Siviter were also extremely helpful with suggestions and information.

On a personal level I'd like to say a huge thank you to my sister Geraldine Hennigan and my wife Joanne for, as ever, being willing to listen and offer helpful suggestions. I'd like to say a big thank you to my sons Thomas and William who, unhindered by being just five and three, were nevertheless willing to proffer critical appraisals! Finally, as always, to those whose stories—be they tragic or otherwise—made this book possible, long may you wander but may it always be at peace.

## PICTURE CREDITS